Choices:

Creating a Financial Services Career

Dr. John W Stolk

Joseph RR Templin

Copyright © 2017

Owned and published by Lamp of Castle Holdings, Inc.

in conjunction with

The Unique Minds Consulting Group, LLC and

The Executive Counsellors Guild.

ISBN 978-1-365-72058-1

LoCH, Inc.
77 East High Street
Ballston Spa, NY, 12020

Choices: Creating a Financial Services Career

Foreword and Appreciations

Table of Contents

WHY? Fill Your Soul…

Work Is NOT a Four Letter Word

Failure Is Your Friend

Review of the Financial Planning Process

Risk Based Planning

SOP's

It's a Trap!

Appendix A: Models

Appendix B: Language Scripts

Appendix C: Resources

Appendix D: Business Planning and Documents

Foreword and Appreciations

Geboren en getogen in Rotterdam, Zuid Holland in het Koninkrijk der Nederlanden,

English Stolk. In English!

Sorry had to switch to my third language English, I mean I was born and raised in Rotterdam, Provence of South-Holland, The Kingdom of the Netherlands. Other than my formal education I also have an DIT (Doctors In Tinkering) and will take anything apart I can get my hands on.

Whether it is changing a timing belt on my Alfa Romeo, repairing a clock, or replacing a well pump at 285 feet, I have no fear. The downside of it is that it sets expectations, my son once said completely stunned "what do you mean you can't fix that"? after he handed me his DS that was in three pieces and looked like it was driven over by a tank.

Insert snide comment about driving a tank here from Joe.

Because the Irish know how to drive?

We know how to make beer. It's more useful than wooden shoes.

Certainly can't cook. Why don't you just boil it some more, it still has some color!

And back and forth it goes. We have been acquaintances for two decades and friends for well over a dozen years at this point, and have spent so much time together we can finish each other's stories in our lectures. This time together has given us a deeper appreciation for what each brings to the table, as well as some synthetic discussions that feature prominently throughout some of the more interesting sections of this book like It's a Trap!

We both have strong business backgrounds, Joe within financial services and John external. This dual approach allows us to ask questions that others wouldn't and develop solutions others can't. If you want to see more about our backgrounds check out our Linkedin profiles:

https://www.linkedin.com/in/drjohnstolk
https://www.linkedin.com/in/joe-templin-685ba4115

We won't bore you with other stuff here, other than Joe would like to thank Dan Leslie from Northwestern for suggesting that we write this book. Also Joe's portions of this are dedicated to his dear friend Rich Kramer, who lost his battle with cancer. If possible, please register as a bone marrow donor.

John says: I specially need to thank Joe for getting my weirdness as someone commented on my LinkedIn profile "John is like a professor who juggles half a dozen ideas for research papers and grant proposals in his mind while giving a highly entertaining lecture on an abstruse subject is a classic example", so bear with me on the pages to follow. If you were to find yourself wondering about how quickly our seminars can have impact, give us a call.

And without further ado, your life will now irrevocably change as your mind is altered. We give you Choices: Creating a Financial Services Career by Dr. John Stolk and Joseph RR Templin, CFP®, CLU, ChFC, CAP (ret).

Fill Your Soul, Not Your Pockets

A special thanks to Gregg Knudten from Thrivent for his feedback on this section. It is people like you that help give us the insight to help more people in the future.

Why why why why why why?

If you spend anytime around young kids, you will hear that question one thousand times an hour it seems. In fact the average four year old asks a question roughly every two minutes. Even a nine-year-old is still asking a question every five minutes. So if you have multiple youngish children like Joe you are literally asked questions non-stop and can't wait for Christmas vacation to be over so you can go to work and have some peace and quiet!

As adults we become know-it-alls, as our knowledge and experience increase our wonder decreases. This is dangerous in that we become hardened in our thinking patterns, and what was once fun and joyous becomes tedious. Play becomes a job, becomes a grind.

Why do we bring this up? Because in building a financial services business there is a lot of hard work. More than you can even comprehend at this point. And disappointment. And heartbreak. But it doesn't matter. Or shouldn't.

Why shouldn't all the negatives that are part of this profession bother you? Because of that why.

What?

No, "Why".

As in "Why am I doing this?", a question you will ask yourself in the most difficult moments of building your future.

If your WHY is big enough, the obstacles in front of you don't matter.

Every athlete has asked themselves "Why am I doing this?" at some point, sometimes while rehabbing from an injury. Almost always around mile 20 in a marathon when their physical and emotional reserves are low and they are ready to give up. This point is the infamous Wall. But to finish the marathon the runners reach down into their guts and pull through it, whether it is pride, or they are raising money in the name of their best friend with cancer, or they know they can succeed because they thrive on the challenge. Their WHYs may be different, but the marathoners all make it through The Wall, or fail to finish. The same is true in our world of financial services.

Your WHY might be to buy a house for your mother that sacrificed everything for you and your siblings.

Your WHY could be because you lost a parent and know the value of what we do, because you have lived it.

Your WHY could be that you want to have a career that lets you have the freedom to take care of a special needs child, or to build a school on another continent to help raise kids from poverty.

You might have become disabled and so know the value of disability insurance.

As Socrates said "The unexamined life is not worth living." The financial services career is the same, because you will have issues, problems, roadblocks on your path. Maybe more than any other career you could chose. Your WHY is what will carry you through.

When that person on the line hangs up on you.

When your significant other yells at you for working so hard and still having no money.

When that client decides to not rollover that million dollars.

When the underwriting comes back as no, no insurance will be issued.

When you spill coffee all over your white shirt to start the day. And the coffee splatters all over your presentation. And the client. That didn't want to meet you anyway.

When your manager reams you out.

When your friends are going out to happy hour and you can't afford to.

When your mom says "we wasted all that money on school just so you could go sell insurance! I thought you were going to go be a physicist with Karl and make me proud." (Yes, direct quote from Joe's mother.)

When your friends are going away on vacation and you can't because you are still in that first twelve months Survival mode of building your business and you can barely take a day and a half off for a weekend.

When it's payday, and not only did you NOT get a check but you owe money for the privilege of working there.

When that person from your training class that you despise just made a huge commission and you know they are too dumb to spell "ETF".

When your significant other says all you do is work and have nothing to show for it and asks if you are having an affair because you are always tired and don't do things together anymore.

When you have no clue how you will pay your rent in four days.

You will go through many of these feelings/situations, and probably dozens more that we can't even comprehend because this will be your unique journey to success, even though it will share some of the same aspects as other's journeys as the archetype of a winner in financial services is pretty well established. We are trying to make sure you understand the price of wealth, of what it takes to build and rule an empire.

Nothing worthwhile is easy.

Nothing truly significant is easy.

But if your WHY is strong enough, none of the above matters. They are not mountains or problems, but merely obstacles to be overcome and reveal your powers as you metamorphasize into something greater and worthy of the treasure. Those who acquire wealth or power or fame without effort can have it taken away from them and become nothing but a warning or a shadowy memory haunting D List reality shows, those who built it themselves are changed forever and can lose everything and come back again. Because those that earned it through sweat and sacrifice of themselves fundamentally change and grow in the process of becoming a success.

"I make of myself a sacrifice to myself" is a line from a 1980's hairmetal song. You will sacrifice yourself to yourself, suffering an unpleasant present for a glorious future. If you can see that vision, believe in it, and can take the pain of growth.

No one can take away our Black Belts that we wear on our souls. The awards are in storage, but the spirit that earned those awards is still burning inside of us and can and will earn different and better awards, because we went through the crucible to become steel. And what carried John and Joe through is their WHY.

We are not allowed to talk much about what Dr. Stolk went through nor his WHY for security reasons. But be glad he is one of the good guys because if he were not it would be very bad. Maybe he will tell you, but only if he wants to because you won't get him to talk if he doesn't want to.

Joe is much more open about his WHY, or WHYs as the case may be. Because after 20+ years in financial services he has obviously evolved. That early 20's ball of fire now has responsibilities for kids and others, and he doesn't bounce back from 80+hour work weeks like he used to. As he writes this paragraph at 4:00 because of the burning fire inside to share with you.

Joe sought out the financial services realm because of a family tragedy. Just before finishing his physics degree from RPI his godfather Royal "Bub" Ribley died unexpectedly with essentially no life insurance and a decades old and out of date will. Because of the fallout from this the family farm where Joe had spent his summers had to be sold. His aunts and uncles stopped talking to each other, his family fractured.

Joe swore that if he could help it that no other family would have to go through the arguments and pain that his family was forced to, to have limited choices in reactive planning when some pro-active planning could have given them options and reduced the emotional pain. It was this belief in what he did that would carry Joe through the early rejections and doubts of his career, that forced him to pick up the phone one more time when he would rather be like the guy in the memes throwing the papers and calling it quits with a string of expletives.

Two years ago Joe sat down with a client that he had done a lot of work with over the years. Some basic life insurance, long term care planning to protect the assets they had accumulated. Investment work, annual tax planning and some pretty important estate planning. The client's wife had died about a year earlier, and the client thanked Joe for all the work that he had done. He would never have to worry about money, could work as he wanted because he enjoyed it, only had to worry about his kids as people, and could do some of the things like take cruises he never could before. The long-term care insurance had helped when his wife had the cancer, and the waiver of premium made it so he was still covered yet didn't have the cost anymore. The client thanked Joe for doing a really professional job and making it so he didn't have to worry at all. **That client was his father.** He was obviously one of the most difficult clients Joe had (partially because of Joe's stubborn mom), but Joe cared about doing the right things for them because he would live with the consequences of the choices. Put yourself in the shoes of your clients' families when you do their planning to give yourself extra incentive.

Over the summer one of Joe's best friends died from leukemia. Rich was 43 years old and had five sons, aged four to fourteen. Rich was godfather to Joe's eldest and Joe is godfather to Rich's first born. Joe has a moral responsibility to those boys and their mother, for they are family by choice as opposed to birth. After the funeral when the friends who had been together for 25 years were talking, the widow turned and said "Thank you Joey. For putting us on the right path back then. The Disability paid during chemo and the life insurance will do what we wanted. The only worry is not financial, but making sure these boys continue to grow into good men as their father was and would want for them."

These are Joe's WHY's. To make sure that farms aren't sold, kids don't leave their neighborhood, and money isn't the main concern. To help people, like his mom taught him.

What is your WHY?

You do not need a family tragedy to be successful in financial services, but those who have experienced one understand the value of what we do on a gut level having lived through it. Intellectual understanding of what we do is important, but it is the emotional dedication that will stand up to the fear and negativity that all new Representatives must fight through early in their career.

One way to reinforce your belief in what you do is to borrow someone else's story. Ask one of the veterans in your office to tell you about the kids that have gone to college because of the work that they have done. Better yet, accompany them when they pay a death or disability claim to feel the raw emotion and appreciation when a check is delivered when it is most needed.

Go with an experienced adviser when they review a client's portfolio and plan that only exist because of what that Representative has done.

Sit there with the client that is still in their home because another planner believed in what they do, and put in place the long term care insurance that is now paying the bills, and you will believe too.

Sales is all about the transfer of belief, and the strongest belief system will generally make the sale.

If you read "Pitch Anything" by Orren Klaff (as we highly recommend), you will understand that belief systems (or as he calls them "frames") are the perceptions of reality, how we "frame" the world around us and our place in it. Either the potential client will sell you, or you will sell them. Who trusts their beliefs more? Whose frame is stronger? The one with the strongest world view that can effectively convey it to the other will make the sale.

The most powerful frame of all is the "moral authority" frame. If you are doing good and right, and believe it completely, you are powerful. More powerful than any intellectual argument, more powerful than weakly held belief systems like "insurance is bad" or "Uncle Sam will take care of me" or "I can deal with retirement once I've had some fun." Transfer your belief to the client and you both win, as only Capitalism can do.

If you cannot experience first-hand the value of what we do as agents of good, look for ways to catch part of the emotion. The Life Insurance Foundation for Education (LIFE) is a non-profit organization that educates consumers on the importance of life and disability insurances. Every year they have the "Real LIFE Stories", a collection of actual insurance clients telling about how the disability insurance saved their company, or how the life insurance on their parents paid for their education and kept the family together. It is absolutely heart wrenching to hear these people talk about the value of what we do. You can watch these at the LIFE website (www.lifehappens.org), and we recommend that you watch at least one of these a week until you truly believe in the good that you do as a financial advisor and will not let a little rejection or ignorance get in your way of helping people protect the people they care about.

Belief in helping people, of working on the side of angels to protect the weak and help them become financially free, is only one component of a strong belief system. **Work on your belief as much as you work on your body and you will be unstoppable.**

The more you help others, the better you will do financially. It is a weird thing in our profession: Financial Advisors that have the most impact, that do the most good, make a ton of money. You will do well by doing good. Working on the side of angels is actually more lucrative and less risky than working for the devil.

A special thank you to Joe's friend Kerry Rudolph, who in a casual conversation threw off the quote "Fill your soul, not your pockets" that summarizes the essence of success for you. Focus on the service part of "financial services", and you will have all the financial rewards you can dream.

Action Item: Get a pad of paper and pen. Lock yourself away from all distraction, whether in a room or at the beach or in the woods, someplace you can have relaxed focus. Write on a piece of paper "WHY Do I Do It?". Start writing.

WORK is NOT a Four-Letter Word

Remember that Dr. Stolk comes from an elite military background. Less than one tenth of one percent of the people that enter the military even qualify to try out for his group, and only about one in ten of those actually complete the training. One out of a hundred people reach black belt, and less than one percent of those make it to the rank we share. Half the people that enter financial services are gone in under a year. Having a little fear to help motivate you is a good thing. But here is the rub: you control your own destiny. Your choices will make you succeed. Nothing else matters.

That's right. YOU and only you determine whether you will be leaving the business or kicking butt in it. Only you. Not your manager, not corporate suits or the market or the Fed or anything else. You. Your choices to win or lose this game.

So lean forward here, and we will give you the secret to success in financial services. The key to a future of interesting challenges, and significant income, and even greater impact on your community. How to be a King or Queen even if not of royal blood. Ready?

WORK.

HARD WORK.

That's it.

Be prepared to work harder and longer than ever before in your life. Many people fail in this career simply because they do not work hard enough. If you are not ready to work your butt off don't even bother to sign up for the licensing class or your contract with your firm, as you will just be wasting everyone's time. Go hard or go home. Sorry about being harsh, but we don't want to see you fail.

If you are not ready to roll up your sleeves and WORK, you will fail.

And really fail: you will peter out and it will suck your soul away and you will go broke and you will dwell in fear until you leave the profession. Then you will say bad things about it because YOU DIDN'T work hard enough. You chose to fail, by not making the choices to work hard and create your financial services career. So make the commitment and follow through on what you need to do to build a successful financial services business. Get ready to bust your butt, but it will be all worth it!!

Let's remind you of a few things.

1. Many people fail out of the financial services field because they don't realize how hard they need to work to succeed.
2. We don't care if you survive or not.
3. We will be brutally honest about everything.
4. Because of 1-3, IF you are ready to work, you will survive and win.

Activity is the Only Guarantee

Activity is the only guarantee of success in financial services. If you follow the Granum Points System, you will understand the truth of what Joe was told by his friend Mark Fine when he was transitioning from a college intern to a full time Representative: If you run 25 points every week on 15 kept appointments like clockwork, you will make so much money you can never spend it all. Well, Mark was wrong. You can find ways to spend it all, if you try hard enough. But you have to work hard at spending it all if you work that much making it.

And another thing is this: if 25 is the minimum threshold of activity to be successful, why just trip over the bar? When you are a young agent, unless you are married and/or have kids, what else do you have to do but work? Why rush out to make Happy Hour at five o'clock when you can work a little bit more and make a ton more money, so that you don't care about two for one drink specials? Wouldn't it make sense to put forth extra effort when you are in your twenties and have energy and enthusiasm and few external constraints to do MORE than the minimum?

One extra appointment scheduled at the end of the day beyond the base level is a 20% increase in activity, which creates a more than 20% increase in cash flow. What are your friends trying to do for a 5% raise, when you can get a 20% or more one so easily?! Wouldn't it be awesome to completely understand and embrace the fact that by keeping one or two more appointments a day for the first few years you are shortening your cycle to success and making sure that you will make more money than anyone you went to school with, even the geniuses and Most Likely to Succeeds? How would you like to be the person buying all of the rounds in a year?! The choice is yours.

It's never crowded along the extra mile.

You have probably heard the statement: **you can be a first year Rep in your first year, or your fifth**. The only way to evolve beyond Inception and Survival is to get the experience of seeing potential clients. Be a first-year Rep only once, get through the pain and uncertainty and being broke quickly by being active so that you can enjoy what is on the other side. Consider it pledging. Or as they say in the country song "If you're going through Hell keep on going."

Think of it this way: Insurance is actuarially based upon the laws of large numbers. Shouldn't your business be too? If you know that only one person out of four that you ask to buy a product from you will do so in the short term, shouldn't you be asking at least twice a day for someone to buy so you have at least a coin flip chance of doing business for the day?

If you know it is a numbers game, shouldn't you have good enough numbers to make sure you succeed? If 25% of the time you win, wouldn't you want to **play enough to make sure you win every single day!**?

People fail in our business because they are just not running enough activity. They don't work hard enough to let the numbers work for them. They are letting luck be a major factor because of small sample size instead of making probability their ally. If you know how to count cards at a black jack table you might lose money on any particular hand or shoe, but at the end of the day you will be profitable if you play enough hands. Exactly the same thing applies to building a financial services practice: any one person may or may not buy from you, but if you see enough people you will by default sell enough to survive and thrive.

Here is an example from baseball because Joe is such a die-hard Yankees fan. To qualify for the batting title, a batter needs to have 502 plate appearances if his team plays the full 162 game regular season. This translates into 3.1 plate appearances per team game for the player. As a newbie to the financial services world you have to keep seven hundred and fifty appointments in your first year. This is 3.1 per day worked. Anything less and you won't qualify for the batting/sales title because you could be cut from the team. Anything below three appointments a day and you might be cut too.

If you keep under a third of this level, less than 250 (a mere five a week, or one per day) your probability of remaining in the business is only in the single digit percentages. Pack your office up now if this is the activity you plan on running. Generally not going to have a long career in financial services in this case. But if you keep at least three appointments per day worked on average, even if they are mainly small cases, you will survive and even thrive in this business because you have achieved your critical threshold of activity.

Early on action is more important than brilliance.

Mickey Straub is the President of SAMUSA, the people that make the green activity tracking calendar books. You should use them. They work. Mickey and Joe have had multiple discussions on the science of success based on activity. And one thing: there are extremely bright lines of activity success.

If you are in your first few years in the business, activity is the single greatest predictor of long range success and wealth. Think about that. Not how good your market is, or what firm you are with, or your IQ or looks. It is purely determined by how much guts you have, how hard you work. Your entire future success is based on your choice, not luck.

If you are keeping under 10 appointments per week on average your probability of being in this field in five years is roughly equal to the number of appointments you keep per week. So if you are seeing less than two potential clients per day on average you either need to be the greatest salesperson in the world or your average revenue per case has to be over ten thousand dollars each to have enough revenue to survive.

Probability is not on your side because you have too small a sample size for success. Here your survival is completely dependent upon being lucky rather than good, and you must continue to be lucky or else you will be out of business because you have not built a skill set and a pipeline to sustain you through the inevitable bad streak.

If you are seeing between 11 and 14 appointments per week (between 2 and 3 a day kept) you have a better chance of writing enough business to stay in the game, but there is still significant inconsistency on a week by week basis in terms of production (and hence cash flow), that could knock you out if you have a multiple week bad string. You might make it through the inevitable rough patch if you have resources to draw from, but a six-week period with no paycheck will kill almost any young Rep's business.

Eleven to fourteen appointments kept per week on average still leaves you vulnerable to these slumps, but you do have the potential for long range success: industry wide numbers show that the number of appointments you keep in an average week in this activity band is roughly one half your survival rate. Thus if you keep 12.5 appointments a week (2.5 a day) you have a one in four shot of surviving your first five years in business. About average overall, but do you chose to be average? Almost three times better than the guys that are seeing less than two people per day, but not a guarantee of success.

But remember: **you** control the number of appointments you schedule, which controls the number of appointments kept. Again, it is YOUR decision to succeed or fail. So you are choosing to make your career more difficult by choosing to not see enough people. Maybe you should make the choice to work a little harder.

Once you cross the three kept per day threshold (15 for a full week), it is almost like magic in that success flips from a possibility to a probability. Long range (5+ year) retention rates are about 50% at 3 kept per day and go up by almost 5% for every appointment over 15 you keep in a week. So at 18-20 kept per week the law of averages is working heavily in your favor instead of against you.

If you can suck it up and really work hard you can actually GUARANTEE success. Guarantee, a word almost illegal in the financial services world. Keep 4 appointments or more on average for six months. The only people we have ever seen leave the profession that were at 4 kept per day (20 a week) or above were for ethical or family reasons. Assuming that you are not an unethical slimebag, **success at 4 kept per day is essentially a guarantee**. That truly should be your goal early in your career. And it can be done if you chose follow what we layout in this book.

Yes, at three or more kept per day there are still the slumps that kill less active advisors, but they tend to be shorter overall because an 0 for 10 closing slump that lasts a month for the under 2 kept per day Representative is under two weeks of failure for a 3 a day Rep. It still hurts and could knock you out of business if the slump extends much further, but momentum should carry you through. Your previous activity helps buy you time, which under active agents do not have.

As Tom Hegna says "The best cure for the blues is activity."

Joe had a stretch at one point where he was 0 for 19 in appointments kept. That was brutal. Actually, it was worse. He was like "Really?! Is EVERYBODY going to cancel?! What did I do to deserve this?" But because Joe ran a hyper active business (33+ selling appointments scheduled per week plus his management responsibilities), this slump although epic only lasted from Monday to Wednesday afternoon of the same week. A less active Representative would have this slump stretch for over an entire week or more just because they would not have the same highly booked schedule. And Joe did keep his next dozen appointments and finished that week with sixteen kept, completing the worst fallout week of his career at 3.1 kept per day. His activity saved him. His worst week of the year was better than an average agent's best week. Not from brilliance, but sheer determination.

Guts are worth more than talent in building your business.

You Are Building a Business, Not Buying a Job

Let's get something crystal clear: you are not in this field to buy yourself a job. It is way too stressful and there is too much risk (of litigation, cash flow uncertainty, market risk, etc.) for you to just try and make a little money here. Either be fully committed to driving this opportunity and making a lot of dough, or don't even enter the field because there are much easier ways to make fifty or seventy thousand dollars a year.

By choosing to be a Financial Representative you are choosing to start with no safety net, no guaranteed income or vacations or benefits.

There are no guarantees other than the ones you earn over time from your efforts.

But you do have total control over how you build your business. There is also no ceiling. You have the potential to literally make more money than anybody you know, on a sustainable basis, without sacrificing your body (like a pro athlete does) or sacrificing your personal life forever (tech start up or doctors).

Look at it this way: you can build a phenomenal business in this field with a minimum amount of invested capital as long as you have desire and work ethic. With under $10K stake you can build a profitable enterprise fairly quickly as opposed to sinking seven figures or more into an operation (like buying a franchise, or building something from scratch) simply by being ready to work hard and follow what we lay out.

You don't have to go to law school or med school or have a 4.0 from the toughest business school out there to be highly successful in financial services.

There are north of a hundred million Americans saying they need more insurance coverage, and few are pleased with their investment guidance right now. The opportunity for you is tremendous. You just have to be ready to work smart and work hard to take advantage of it. Keep the three plus appointments per day that we talked about and within two years you will be making six figures. Keep that level of investment into your business going and in five years you will have great income, flexibility in your schedule, and the life that is the envy of those that did not decide to work hard.

Start Up Success

Just like any start up business you need to be mentally, physically, and financially prepared to work your butt off. Instead of Joe and John telling you how hard you need to work and the mindset you need to adopt, we think it makes more sense to give examples and quote directly from a cross section of our clients that have "been there, done that".

1. **The New Attorney.** Many of Joe's clients were young attorneys, and there are many parallels between an associate in law building their practice and a financial services professional building theirs. The biggest advantage that attorneys have coming out of law school versus you is that they know without a doubt that their critical threshold of activity is 2,000 billable hours. This is not two thousand hours of work like a normal full time employee has: this is forty hours a week on average of work directly attributable to a client that can be coded and billed to them. This generally requires 1.5 times that in total time to achieve, or sixty-hour work weeks. And this is the minimum. The ones that build a great career know they need to sacrifice the first few years, often putting in 80 hour weeks to make partner. If you work this hard for the first few years you will achieve more than you ever thought possible, and you will have earned every iota of it. New accountants generally are pretty close to this sixty-hour week baseline too, but most of their crunch time is during tax season when they put in six or even seven day weeks. Yet over a year a young accountant will average right about two thousand billable hours, plus whatever it takes to get this (marketing time, prep time, continuing education, firm meetings, etc.). These are the two closest professions to financial planning out there. So look directly at them to see what they have to do to be successful early in their career because you as a professional in financial services need to be

doing THE EXACT SAME THING early on. Long range because of the residual income we can achieve you actually get much more freedom and compensation than these peer professionals do, but early on they have base salaries and time off that you don't. So how come they are outworking you?

2. **Half Days**. Joe's father built one of the leading healthcare consulting firms in the country from scratch. And his secret as revealed to his son? **"Work half days. Any twelve hours will do."** Twelve hours a day, five days a week equates to sixty hours a week, directly aligned with what is expected of the new attorney discussed above. Funny how analogous it is. And reviewing his activity from his first few years of full time activity as a financial advisor, Joe worked about that many hours a week (exclusive of studying for his letters and practicing his craft, which added the additional twelve hours a week he averaged in the first five years). So be ready to work half days, any twelve hours you chose. The nice thing is that these half days don't last. After four or five years you have built a business with residual income, repeat sales, and staff to take care of the non-client facing responsibilities so you can start working less while continuing to see your income climb. By the time you are a decade into this career you will be taking several weeks a year of vacation and working LESS hours than your friends because you have built a business. By five years in you will be working only 10 hour days, and at a decade you will have earned the right to work a "normal" forty-five hour week. But you need to earn that right by working half days to start.

3. **Tech Start Up.** Many of our corporate level clients were tech start-up companies. Unlike the young professionals from above, these guys did not have the safety nets of the well-funded organization that has been around for decades to draw from, just like you don't as you start your career. So they had

to really hump it and make it happen, and were living on a shoestring while building their business. They had the same uncertainty that you have for the future, but were doing so without the guidebook you are holding. They truly took risk while you just need to make a tradeoff of time for wealth. Joe has recently built several new start-up companies, and the adrenaline rush of every day creating something is both addicting but draining over time. Easier to create something in your 20's than in your 40's with three hooligan kids that demand your time, and a mortgage, and all the other demands on your time.

4. **Hearing is Believing** Some quotes that directly apply to what you are going to do in terms of sacrificing to build your business, taken from our clients, might inspire you. They are not intended to scare you, but to give you a realistic understanding of the hardships you will face and the rewards that await you once you have built an MDRT level business. These quotes are from clients both within the financial services world and outside of it but all are insightful.

A. "I slept in my office because I couldn't afford an apartment for the first six months."

B. "We rented a cheap run down house, slept four guys to a room in two rooms, and the rest of the house was the office. No commuting costs, we could work constantly and sleep when need be, and had the peer pressure to succeed since we were all in it together was really beneficial."

C. "Having no money and no guarantee of success scared the shit out of me. I worked all the time out of fear. Fear of failing, fear of embarrassment, fear of having to go home and tell my father that I hadn't made it. And now he brags about how successful I am."

D. "When I first started I kept my crappy apartment from grad school because I knew I would never be there. All I did was work, study, and go to the gym for the first six months of my career. I kept that place for the first 2 years of my business and saved a ton of money since I didn't have a phone or cable since I would never be around to use them."

E. "My friends took the easy corporate route and had vacations in the first year and knew what their paycheck was going to be. I didn't. I struggled. I built my own corporation because I believed in what I was doing. And I was never downsized, or had to report to an idiot manager. Yes, I had sleepless nights and missed out on some fun in my mid-twenties. But now I make more money than all of them combined and take time off whenever I want. The only idiot boss I have to deal with is me!"

F. "I wish I had started my career five years earlier, before I had kids so that I could work more and make more. It really limited my business to only be able to work eight or nine hours a day because of the time needs of the family. I am doing well now, but I wish I could have worked harder earlier."

G. "Ramen was my friend. Any cash I had was plowed into the business for the first two years. I struggled but worked my way through it, and now I make more money than any of my friends, even the smart ones."

H. "Starting my insurance career, I had only my ability to work hard and do as I was told. I did both, and now I make more in a quarter than my parents did in a year."

I. "If you had told me a decade ago I would be driving a Benz today I would have said you were insane. But the work ethic I got on the farm, applied to doing financial planning, has made me more successful than any of my friends in engineering ever will be."

J. "Every day I go home exhausted. But it feels good because I am building a business for me, not working to make some old guy even richer."

K. "I chose to sacrifice my twenties to build my business and enjoy the rest of my life. My friends that had a blast in their twenties are going to have to sacrifice for the rest of their lives."

And that is why you want to bust your hump for the first several years of your financial sales career, because you can and the results all accrue to you. As Joe was told on the first day of his training with Northwestern Mutual **"To live like a king you have to work like a slave**." Adopt this mentality for the first few years and you will have a great kingdom and palace soon enough!

Running the Marathon

We have often heard that a career in financial services is like running a marathon: a long range focus is needed, there is a ton of work and sacrifice, and few people have the will to do it. But just like not everyone can be an elite 2:15 marathoner, not everyone will be a million dollar a year producer. Does that mean you don't try? Every person that completes the marathon gets a medal, whether you do it in 2:15 or 5:12. You are still a marathoner. Joe has his medals in his office to remind him of the miles he slogged through and it reinforces his faith in the activity for success in financial services. He was definitely not among the fastest marathoners, but he has still completed multiple marathons and Ragnars (200ish mile team relay races). You are probably faster than he is, but how many marathons have you done? Do you put forth the effort EVERY DAY?

Just getting off the couch and making a committed effort to do a marathon separates you from the majority of Americans. Get off the couch and make the same sort of commitment to your financial services career. Put in the effort. Run the miles in the dark before work, and don't stay out all night partying with your friends because you are trying to do something great. Something many of your friends don't understand or are unwilling to work for.

Run your business hard to get the rewards that are at the finish line of every pay cycle. Also, running physically is a great idea because of the mental and physical stamina it creates. We have seen financial advisors who plateau because they physically cannot handle working more than five or six hours a day. If you have a health concern that limits you like this so be it, but the average new financial advisor typically is in their early twenties with some form of athletics in their background. So keep being athletic, even if it is only a few hours a week because it will directly impact your success in this field.

Sir Richard Branson when asked the single greatest tool to influence productivity said **"Work out more."** The man is worth a few billion dollars, primarily from companies that he has built. Maybe you should listen to him on this.

John and Joe use martial arts as their primary physical training to increase their productivity. Both of us are martial artists, specifically in Tae Kwon Do. Martial arts actually have a direct link to success in financial services because of the focus on repetition to perfect technique and a competition mindset, combined with superior mental focus, endurance, and confidence.

Having faced and repeatedly defeated fear in the dojang (training hall) gives martial artists a distinct advantage with financial sales. Anything from aikido to karate or tai chi will give you the mental acuity and physical abilities to supplement this book and your other training to maximize your production. We just happen to both be Tae Kwon Do stylists (with some boxing and judo and other things mixed in), but there is a martial arts system out there that fits your body and desires that we suggest you adopt to make yourself better on multiple levels. Martial arts will teach you to master techniques and fear, two key attributes of top level producers.

We refer to high activity as the key to success, and it is not just limited to when you have a jacket on.

Be active outside the office and you will be more active within it.

As we acknowledged earlier, the majority of the people who decide to become financial Representatives have athletics in their background, and this is good because you have been exposed to work ethics and losing in addition to playing the game the right way. And you have learned teamwork.

Unfortunately, when you start your career there is no team. There is you, and you alone. Yes, you will have managers and peers and maybe some office support staff to potentially help you out, but in the end it is you. You will win or lose on your own. So hone your skills to maximize the chance of success in every opportunity you are presented, and maximize the number of chances you get to succeed. Furthermore, do not rest on your laurels: **just because you won your last game doesn't mean anything in the current one.**

The story of the former champ that got sedentary and lazy and was defeated by the young and hungry competitor is common. Do not become complacent in your success. The secret of success in financial planning for the first few years is this: work your butt off, both inside the office and outside of it. If you do that you will survive the early years and reap the rewards in the future.

Failure is Your Friend

You are going to fail in this business. Get used to it, embrace it. We hope you were told this before you decided to enter this field, but management probably "didn't want to scare you" (as we have been told by several offices) and sugar coated it by just talking about the upside potential. Better for you to hear the cold hard truth before it blindsides you. You are going to fail.

You are going to fail in this business every single day, hopefully multiple times. And that is a good thing. Quick: who is the non-steroids tainted Home Run King of Major League Baseball? That's right, Hammerin' Hank Aaron with 762 home runs. Did you realize that he had almost TWICE as many strike outs as home runs? That he NEVER hit 50 home runs in a season, but had more 30 HR seasons than anyone else and hit 24 or more for over fifteen seasons in a row?! Consistent effort and production leads to a Hall of Fame career. Even the greatest hitters ever (Cobb, Williams, Ruth) failed to get on base over half the time. Getting a successful hit three times out of ten is a Hall of Fame pace as long as you do it enough. Every single baseball player who has had enough opportunities (plate appearances) that their output cannot be attributed to pure dumb luck (or better hitting through chemistry like Bonds) has failed at a significant rate. As will you.

Wayne Gretzky, the Great One, is arguably the greatest hockey player of all time. He said "You miss 100% of the shots you don't take."

Maybe you prefer basketball. To quote Michael Jordan on failure "I've missed more than 9000 shots in my career. I've lost almost 300 games. 26 times, I've been trusted to take the game winning shot and missed. I've failed over and over and over again in my life. And that is why I succeed." Be like Mike.

Failure must become your frenemy. You must embrace it, hate it with a passion, but have no fear of it. You must learn to accept failure and turn it into fuel for success.

Most of the people you ask to take action will not do so. Traditionally only about 25-35% of the people you attempt to sell will ultimately become clients of yours, meaning two thirds of the time you are going to be rejected. And that is tough for many people to swallow, especially those of the Millennial Generation that were insulated from failure from the time that they played soccer but didn't keep score and everyone got a trophy up through high school and college where everyone got at least a B because all are above average. Sorry, the world doesn't care about your special snowflake feelings.

Learn to lose, and to hate it but accept it. The constant rejection is one thing that breaks many new agents. But if you have the fortitude to take it, the thick skin and the belief in what you do, when you do succeed is worth it, both emotionally and financially. You are about to commit to a lifetime of rejection, of having people say "No, I don't want to do the right thing for myself and my family." You need to develop the ability to deal with it or else you are going to be under your desk crying and sucking your thumb and out of the business.

BUT....IF you can deal with being told **NO**, of failing two to three times as many times as you succeed, of being able to after being rejected say "Next", then you will be tremendously successful. Adversity creates excellence, and you will face adversity every day for the rest of your professional life. **"Successful people do what unsuccessful cannot or will not"** is something that has been bandied about the financial services world for decades and it is absolutely true. No, you will not succeed with every client, but if you have the courage and work ethic and strong enough WHY to face enough rejections you will get enough **"YES's"** to make it worth your while. If you can deal with the glass being not three quarters empty but a fourth full of really good stuff, and you have enough glasses, you will be very happy in the end.

So now that you know that you will fail and should fail, you need to realize that the more you fail the more you succeed, that every "NO" on average gets you closer to a "YES". Insurance is based upon the law of large numbers, so the more attempts you have the more successes you have. So **fail and fail often**! Strike out at the plate with the client because on average you will get a hit just under one time out of three (a Hall of Fame pace over the long run), but make sure you go down swinging and not looking with the bat on your shoulder. Take your best shot, because the worst thing that could happen is they say "No" and you say "Next" and move on. **Their loss, not yours.**

So let's now focus on the failure milestones you should pass on your journey towards building a financial services business you can be proud of. We don't care if you have been in the business for a few years and are struggling, have just started and passed your licensing exams, or are a 20 year experienced producer that wants to radically change and grow. Anyone that is in the financial planning arena that wants to have great forward success needs to forget the pain of failures of the past and be ready to move forward, failing often but always advancing.

In your **next five days** you should pick up the phone enough times to strike out 100 times, to be told "NO" by 100 different people. This is going to be among the most difficult things that you do in your entire career because you are not accustomed to failing yet and this is a LOT of failure over a very short period of time. If you are more experienced you might have had this many NO's but not this quickly nor from people that you actually have some relation with.

Don't despair! Because after you fail spectacularly in that first week you are actually in the business and will start keeping appointments and seeing people. And selling, which leads to making money. But you have to be rejected to get to this point, to get to the people that you can help. If you fail 100 times to get an appointment (referred leads or warm relationships to begin with), you will get in the neighborhood of 75-80 successes, meaning new appointments scheduled to begin your sales process with these prospective clients.

We actually recommend getting two rolls of pennies and setting them out on your desk. Every time you get a NO take a penny off the desk and put it in a jar. Whenever you get a YES put something else on the desk, like a dollar bill (fake $1,000 bill is better) or a poker chip or a green 3x5 card. Some positive visualization, because it will reinforce that NO's lead to YES's and all those penny failures are actually dollar successes.

If you do not get 100 NO's in your first week of phoning, you are either an unnaturally gifted person and had over 75% of the people tell you YES, or you did not pick up the phone enough. Don't lie to yourself on the numbers as you are only damaging your future earnings. If you are under a year in the business and did not get 100 genuine NO's (and the YES's that go with it), we will bet $500 you will be out of business in a year because the vast majority of those that don't get enough NO's in the first week are going to be gone.

Not that we are mean, it is just the math based on tens and hundreds of thousands of previous people that have entered the industry and not worked hard enough at the beginning. **Believe in math, because it is cold and doesn't care about you.**

NOTE: if you are going to be stubborn and insist on cold calling, you need to fail 100 times on the phone A DAY FOREVER to be able to get the activity needed for success. We are pretty tough guys, but even we learned that getting punched in the mouth all the time when there are ways to avoid it is probably not a good idea. Get out of cold calling as quickly as you can, as there are just so much more effective ways to build a business. Or you can keep trying to knock down that stone wall with your thick head. Your choice, just like almost everything in this career.

So after you fail one hundred times in that first week to get an appointment you can then fail at this a little less often. If you failed 100x in the first week, now you only need to fail that often over the next month to keep you schedule full and be active. That is a ton less pain than what you just went through, isn't it? Because you are now mentally tougher than you were, one of the key characteristics of those that succeed in financial services. These 100 NO's will equate to around 100 successes as your skills improve, and quickly you will start getting extremely busy and have to ramp this back even further because you are actually succeeding. Failing often and quickly makes you reach success in a hurry. **Run through the fire, don't walk.**

You could decide to fail less often, which means you will succeed less often. Every NO in phoning will yield about one Yes on average early in your career, so the quicker you get a hundred NO's the quicker you will get 100 Yeses. Those attempting to sell you on this spectacular career too often only focus on the positive, and you need to understand the negatives to be able to work through them.

NO gets you to Yes.

More NO's get you to more Yeses.

It is a bizarre way to work, focusing on failure to succeed but is actually what professional athletes and professional investors do, so it might make sense to adopt their approach here. After getting told "NO" one hundred times a month you can pull back even further, to one hundred "NO's" a quarter which will equate to a bit over 120 new appointments scheduled, or a bit over two per business day as your skills improve. Continuously running at this level of up front activity for the first few years will guarantee a successful and sustainable career, so get used to getting those "NO's" and start chalking up those strike outs!

The next focus after that first month is to getting prospective clients to say "NO!" to your face. This is tougher because just having someone reject you on the phone whom you have never met is not that big of a deal compared with someone that you have met face to face and interacted with and given guidance and recommendations telling you "NO".

But now that you are starting to get used to the feeling of failing regularly you'll be OK, because you know that failure leads to success. So now you need 100 prospective clients to tell you "No, I do not want to buy what you are suggesting to take care of myself or my family."

A few weeks earlier in your career this could overwhelm you mentally, but now you understand that it is a numbers game, and for every two to three people that say NO one says "Yes, I want to be responsible and follow your recommendation and buy this financial product to achieve our goals." Meaning those 100 failures will yield between twenty-five and forty sales. Which is two or more times what the average new agent does total in their all too short careers.

Focusing on failing enough times will guarantee that you don't fail out of the business.

Having someone decide to not buy from you hurts mentally and emotionally. You have invested a few hours in getting to know this person or family, crunched some numbers and done some projections so you know that based on what they want to achieve, they need whatever you are recommending. You have sat there and talked about their dreams and fears. You know more intimate details about them than their family does, than their best friend does. You are trying to do it for their benefit more than yours, and when you are unable to communicate it or they opt to not take care of their family obligations it hurts.

You have become emotionally invested in them and their future, and when they don't do what you know is right it can feel like a slap in the face. You need to understand that as long as you have done your best in terms of discussing with them what they want and laying it out for them, it is a THEM problem, not a YOU problem. You cannot always get the hit; even when you do everything absolutely right you might hit the ball hard right at the fielder.

The potential client ultimately makes the choice and they can chose poorly and not listen to you. Learn from it and move on, it is their decision to not do what they should do for their future. You are doing what you should for theirs, and not everyone makes as good choices as we do. Don't let their poor choice affect how you work with the next client, and the next, and the next.

There are numbers from a variety of sources (Northwestern Mutual, LIMRA, et al) that show if you sell at least fifty policies in your first year you have at least a coin flip chance of still being in the profession five years later. If you sell that many in about half the time in a sustainable manner like we are showing you to do, you essentially guarantee yourself success. You will not fail long range if you fail enough early.

The outcome of intelligent failure is success.

If you are primarily investments, focus getting told NO 100 times anyway, because you will open over 100 accounts. Don't forget the insurances that should accompany these clients planning either.

Once you have failed one hundred times to get the client to do what they should to ensure their dreams, keep focusing on failing. Keep striking out on selling financial products one hundred times a quarter from this point on and you will without any doubt evolve through the next several levels of success and ultimately completely control your own financial destiny. One of the biggest agents in the history of the Northwestern Mutual years ago said that his focus was to lead his

Agency every month in "NO's", because he knew from the numbers that he would be getting more than enough "Yeses" to achieve his goals.

If you fail 100 times a quarter you will sell somewhere around 150 policies (200+ investment accounts) a year, which means that over a dozen times a month you win. And there is NO ONE in the insurance world that sells a dozen policies a month that ultimately loses. Nor investment advisors doing 200 new accounts a year.

Failure leads to winning, and the more you fail in the end the more you win.

So after you fail on the phone a hundred times in a week, and then in a month, then fail to sell insurance or other financial products to 100 clients as quickly as you can. If you do so in under four months, you have a very high probability of continuing to fail regularly for many decades into the future. Which means you will succeed at a tremendous rate. **Embrace failure as part of your profession the way that a professional athlete does**.

Some point between your one hundred failures to sell products and your retirement decades later you will hit the $100K premium/investment gross commissions threshold, probably within the first eight to twelve months of your business if you continue to maintain the activity levels described earlier. And this is a critical point. When you hit $100K of premium (or investment gross if you are mainly an asset accumulation person), you have probably earned around $75K to $90K total. Not too shabby, but not that great either. You are working way too hard to only make six or seven thousand dollars a month, but it is a good start. Unless you live in a major metro area (NYC, LA, Chicago, etc.) you can live on $90K before business expenses a year as long as you are single. You will be making more than most of the people you went to school with. It is a good minimum standard. But it is only a base standard not your ultimate goal, because there are easier ways to make this amount of money without the stress that we go through in financial services. But if and when you hit this $100K level of production you should be congratulated because you are now truly in the financial services business!

If you keep having faith in your systems and the processes that got you to where you are and keep running them at the level you have, you will keep growing. The $100K of premium/gross will then become $100K of revenue, placing you in the top quartile of all Americans.

And then that $100K of revenue will become $100K of income to you net of the business expenses, which is a great place to be.

And then $100K of after tax income after running your business and paying Uncle Sam. You are really doing something once you have evolved to this level of production. You will have built and be running a business that is doing significant good in the world, and being well compensated for it.

You forcing yourself to fail will help others succeed, and lead to your own success. Your 100 strikeouts will lead to one hundred K of cash flow. Less failures means you will make less money. Do you like money? Because we sure do! That is why we make a choice that others don't understand: we chose to work hard and face rejection.

The more we hear NO the more we hear Yes.

Fail your way to success. Fail often, fail fast, and fail forward.

After Action Assessment:

After every military operation there is an after action assessment. It is more than a debriefing, it is an analysis of what occurred. It allows for the capturing of information and distilling it into knowledge and wisdom for future missions. Whether a failure or a success, there is valuable intel.

Think about how to apply this to your business, so that every loss is actually a lesson and every win is a dual win in that you get compensated AND get better for next time.

The Planning Cycle

The days of Tom Cruise calling Gordon Gecko on the phone and getting $100k to invest just on his word over the phone are gone. Who knows what is going to shake out of the DoL Fiduciary Standard rules under Trump, but it is intuitively obvious to the most casual of observers that to build a sustainable and profitable financial services business you should take a process driven approach. Or you can go back to the 1980's for a purely sales driven approach, but then you need big hair and skinny ties and dangly earrings and have to listen to Debbie Gibson singing in the mall. Trust us, a modern process driven approach is better for all involved.

Both of us have engineering backgrounds, so having a process that can be repeated over and over and over again with predictable results and quality is near and dear to our hearts. And your Compliance Officer will love if you have a documented and replicated process, because it will make their life easy and make sure that you meet your firm's need to cover their behind. Plus you will probably make more money, and definitely have less stress. Why?

Cycles repeat. Great businesses are built off of having a repetitive production process that can be maximized for efficiency. Following a planning process that you use EVERY time, with EVERY client will dramatically increase your efficiency. This will allow you to make more money in less time. It will allow you to predict your revenues with greater clarity, and as you build up staff to run your organization they will appreciate the controls on the chaos that is natural in our world.

Process >>> Product

What do you sell?

Is it mainly accumulation tools like mutual funds, whether exposed or in a tax shield like a 401k or 529? Are you slinging Long Term Care Insurance left and right? Annuity Agent?

Guess what? To quote that great American leader The Rock: It doesn't matter!

In the end you have to sell two things: your process, and yourself.

Let's repeat that. You sell your financial planning process. And you sell yourself. Any stocks or bonds or policies or what not are secondary, and if they do not buy **you** they are not buying anything FROM you.

At other points in this book we will address maximizing your individual value, but for now let's focus on the process that adds value and reveals to your potential clients the value you bring to them. It will make you look good, and make them aware of the needs that ultimately you will fill with products of various forms.

So let's talk about SOP's. If you were a military person you'd say "ah, Standard Operating Procedures. The way we do it." And if you aren't a military person or engineer, you now know what an SOP is.

Think of McDonalds. They may or may not really make food in your opinion, but a few years back they were actually almost moved from the restaurant sector to the manufacturing sector for economic analysis reasons, because they literally are an assembly line. It is the secret to the McDonalds franchise, and a new franchisee has to attend Hamburger U and do it their way, every time, or else they give up their franchise. Something your manager would love to impose on you because they could predict the bottom line and have zero compliance issues. The exact reasons why you should follow SOP's like a fanatic. McD's used to say "Billions Served". Wouldn't you like billions managed? You need a process so the millionth dollar and the billionth are processed in essentially the same way, or else you will remain an artisan hamburger maker that has a nice little business but no scalability.

If you have not recently read Michael Gerber's "The E Myth Revisited" you might want to do so to reinforce the value of a process driven business.

So here without much ado is the financial planning process Joe used. He was a consistent Million Dollar Round Table producer from it and had the free time to do volunteer work and run marathons and fight in the World Championships as well as recruit and develop almost 100 Reps, so it works.

Sometimes we will call it the sales cycle, or the planning process, or other things along those lines. Doesn't matter what you call it as long as you follow it. Just like harvesting crops can only follow the plowing and sowing of the fields, then the nurturing of the crops in their natural order, so too does selling financial products naturally follow fact finding and problem discovery and closing. It is the natural order of things, and when you try to violate the natural order you create chaos and abominations. Embrace and adopt the sales cycle, trust in it and you will be well served because your activities will naturally lead to sales and success.

If you have read Al Granum's books such as The Art and Science of Client Building this should be familiar to you, as it will be if you have read our book "Do You Want To Make MDRT, or Not?" If you haven't read that book you might want to get yourself a copy now from Amazon or the Unique Minds website (www.unique-minds.com) as strong fundamentals mean greater long range growth.

Also, you need to keep track of your activity numbers and ratios like you are a booky and your life depends on it. Because your career does. We like the SAMUSA green book and online scorecard. Mickey Straub and his team have done a really good job, and keeping track of your stats will give you a competitive advantage. www.samusa.com

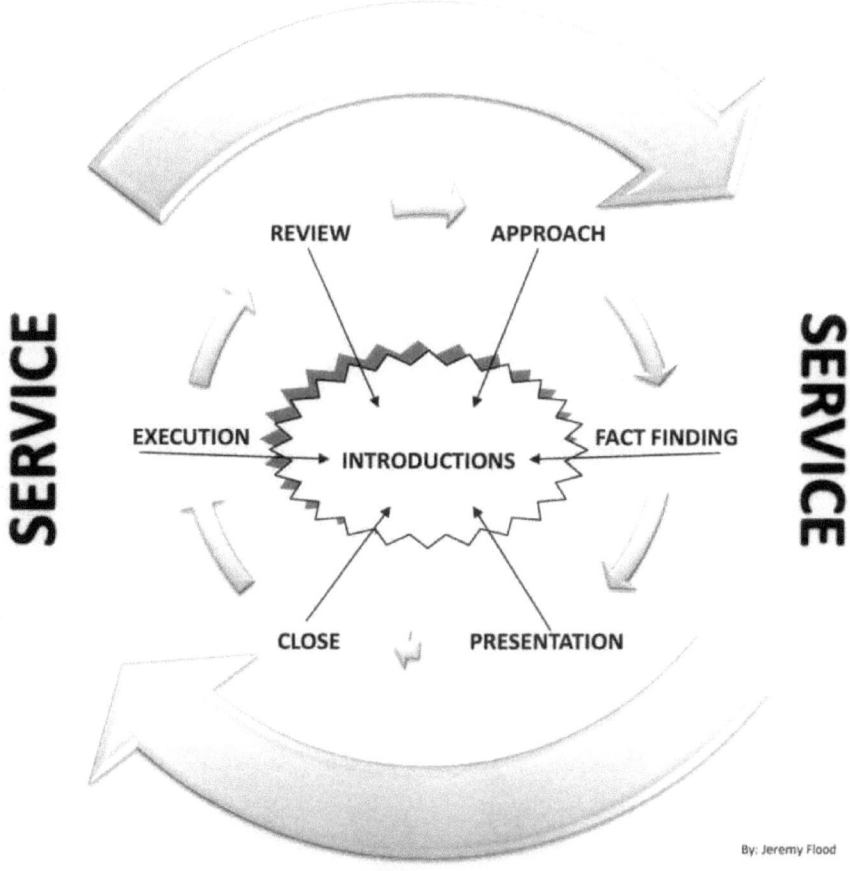

SERVICE

SERVICE

REVIEW   APPROACH

EXECUTION   FACT FINDING

INTRODUCTIONS

CLOSE   PRESENTATION

By: Jeremy Flood

Internalize the planning process and embrace it for maximum success. Deviation leads to errors. Errors lead to mistakes. Mistakes lead to lawsuits. Lawsuits lead to headaches and more paperwork and all sorts of not fun things.

Step One: Set Appointment

Phoning is the hardest part of the sales cycle because it involves the greatest amount of rejection. If you do not get appointments, you will not be able to talk to people. You will not be able to take them through your planning cycle. You will end up having to go and get a job that sucks your soul away a little bit, day by day and week by week until you are middle aged and driving kids to soccer practice in a used mini van and wondering why you are depressed. Because you didn't pick up the phone and take control of your destiny, because you were afraid someone on the other end of the line would be mean to you.

Let's talk about cold calling for a minute though.

It sucks. It is horrifying. It is the reason why many people give up on this career because after the 50th time of having someone hang up on you in a day you start to question yourself, and by the 500th time you have been beaten down. Oh, and of those 500 calls, maybe one or two will meet with you so you can actually take them through your financial planning process. It is so inefficient, yet still too many firms and individuals still do it.

Look, if you are going to call the investment bankers on Wall Street because they have money, don't you think every other new financial advisor within two hundred miles has the same idea? They are probably buying the same list as you and calling these people too. These Wall Street bankers (or physicians, or attorneys, or whichever high income group you want to substitute) are being called 50 times a day so are getting really good at saying NO to everyone. Don't even waste your time doing it.

To make 500 cold calls probably takes an entire business day. Wouldn't it make more sense to do a little research, build a few short lists, and work to get referrals to call? Same one day of work, but orders of magnitude greater results, plus you'll still have some dignity and soul left. We will address this more later. Just don't cold call as the main way to build your business. Serious. Just. Don't.

Instead of now giving you Joe's awesome phoning language that lead him to get 90% of the people he talked with to schedule appointments, we are going to assume that you understand the importance of having your language down so that it is completely natural to you. Having it so ingrained as to be automatic is similar to an athlete having their fundamental skills in muscle memory: they can react faster and better than their opponents. Practice that much, not just your phoning language but all parts of your sales cycle to maximize your business.

Remember that your attitude must be that they will meet with you because everyone meets with you. Confidence comes through the line. This attitude and belief cannot be understated: **confidence is attractive**, and belief in yourself will make others believe in you. So do not be a weak and wimpy beggar on the phone because you will then come to hate dialing because no one meets with a weakling. The phone call from you to start the financial planning process could be the single most important phone call of their life. So be not afraid, you are awesome and they should be thanking you for the opportunity to work with you.

The Approach

The Approach is what you say in the first few minutes of your first interaction with a potential client when you are actually initiating the financial planning process. Don't focus on the fish on the wall or other BS. You have roughly 8 seconds for them to size you up and have a gut reaction of continuing to talk to you or not. Don't waste it with mindless blabber.

Yes, people do business with those they like and respect. But more important than being liked is being respected, and respect begins the instant that you open up the dialogue about helping them achieve their financial goals.

Our experience and research has shown that small talk is for the small minded. Successful people are busy and have more important (in their mind) things to do than chit chat with you. Show respect for this and demand the same for yourself. You have under 10 seconds to make them want to talk to you, and you need to triage them to see if they are serious about working with you or not. This is not to be cold blooded, but you aren't getting paid to sit there and have tea and crumpets. If you and this potential client hit it off there is always time to go get a cocktail down the road once you are moving along in your business relationship. But you need to determine quickly if they are going to take your time with no return on investment for you, or if they are a jerk that will make you want to poke out your own eyes with a butter knife. **Successful people respect professional efficiency.**

Again, instead of giving you Joe's language right now we will skip ahead in the process. You can find the language in the Appendix, or in "Do You Want To Make MDRT, or Not?".

One thing we will reinforce here though is that the approach is the foundation of the professional relationship. You get to set the ground rules of the engagement right here and now. So tell them you work on a referral basis. Get their agreement on this, because if you don't do so NOW, you will be scrambling later in the planning process to get introduced to other people. That sucks. Period case closed. Upfront contract with the client: "when I create value for you, part of the way you are going to pay me is introductions to other high quality people like yourself, just like so and so introduced us." If you don't do so you will miss out on a tremendous amount of money and create extra work for yourself later.

Fact Finding

The Approach should naturally lead into Fact Finding. Fact Finding is the step in the financial planning process where you get to gather the information that is critical to serve your client. More importantly it is the starting point of your RELATIONSHIP with them, a meeting of mutual discovery where you will get:

1. Data

2. Feelings

3. Philosophies

Presentation

The goal of the Presentation stage is two-fold, it is meant for Education and Motivation, and each is important. This is the stage in the planning process where you present your analysis and recommendations to the potential client, where you get a chance to show your knowledge and get them not only aware of the shortfalls of their current planning but ready to take action to change their future outcomes.

Execution: We break out Execution into a completely different step in the planning process even though it is the logical extension of a presentation if everything that has come before it was done correctly and the client is properly motivated.

Execution is the paperwork step. Build staff to do this for you because you are not paid to fill out paperwork. Hire the person for $25 or $50 an hour to do this so you can go do $200+ per hour planning instead of checking boxes on a form and making photocopies.

Review: Change is constant. Your clients will get married (and almost half will divorce), maybe have kids. Employment will change. They are depending upon you to help them through their life changes, as well as the ones imposed by Washington, and the markets. You should review the planning and situations with your clients (or at least give them the option to do so) every six months or whenever there is a "life changing event".

Introductions: Introductions are the fuel for your financial planning machine. If you stop feeding the machine it will eventually stop.

You need to train your clients to feed your machine with new introductions every time you interact and add value to them. Do not fall into the trap of only asking for them after a client has bought a product from you as you will not survive in the business if you do so. If you want to get more introductions on a systematic basis, go now to www.introductionmachine.com for a tech based supplement to what you are already doing. Also look in the Appendix for additional language and tactics to acquire the Introductions you deserve.

Process is more important than product. Master your process and you will sell enough product to have a great business.

Risk Based Products

We get it. You are an "Investment Advisor" or "Financial Advisor" or a "Financial Planner". That's great. But if you ignore the risk based needs of your clients you are doing them a disservice. You are endangering all the work you have done on the accumulation side, and you are opening yourself (rightly) to lawsuits.

If you are licensed to sell investments I almost guarantee you are also licensed to sell risk based products like life insurance and long term care coverage. And your manager and Home Office want you to do so too. Why?

Insurances give you a big time revenue bump short term, then long trails. Investments give you long range income and growth. Just like your clients need both to build a complete financial plan, you need both to build a complete financial services business.

Insurance is not a religion. It is a tool. You have no problem using a 529 Plan to help with a client's educational planning, why wouldn't you use a 7702 Plan because it has less volatility and has lower reporting requirements for financial aid? Oh, you haven't heard of a 7702 Plan? That is the Internal Revenue Code section defining Life Insurance. Maybe you should read it after you read this section of the book so that you can serve your clients properly while also building a more balanced business.

We are going to do a quick overview of the major human risk based products and some reasoning behind including them in your planning for clients. There are numerous specialists out there to assist you in specific areas (such as our good friend Corey Anderson, The DI Geek. His number is 888-700-GEEK. Talk about good marketing!). Instead of becoming an expert, understand the basics and delegate to another, learning from them in the process until you can handle most things on your own and bring the insurance component in-house.

Life Insurance:

Term Insurance:

Today term insurance is pretty easy to understand: you pay money to the insurance company (the premium) and if you die while the term is in force (a term of X years or until a certain age, as long as you pay) then they pay the named beneficiary the amount specified. Simple. Originally no underwriting until (as Stolk will always point out) the Dutch started taking into account factors like age and occupation. That was the beginning of truly modern life insurance.

Now they use actuarial science and a ton of data to determine prices. Smoking is the worst thing you can do, because from a medical point of view it is almost guaranteed to screw you up big time. And kill you earlier. So you pay more. Same for health issues like diabetes or cancer or being overweight: all of these drive the price up to a lesser extent. And unlike health insurance, the insurance company can say "nope, too great of a risk. We won't give this person insurance."

But once they give it to your client the Company can't yank it away, unless they stop selling it in your state, give up that entire line of business, client gets past the term that they guarantee, or your client doesn't pay the premium. Term insurance is by far the most cost effective way to buy a lot of life insurance for a limited amount of money for a limited amount of time. You should sell boatloads of coverage because that is what your clients really need and term insurance is so damn cheap at this point the only reason your client doesn't have enough is because you didn't do your job as their planner.

In many ways term insurance is a commodity, because if you are dead (which is when they pay), there is no dispute of said fact. There are some variations with the period guaranteed and the rates, as well as some of the side benefits like convertability to permanent coverage and disability waiver of premium (where they pay your premiums and keep policy in force if you become disabled). Term insurance is so damn cheap at this point there is no reason to not have enough coverage, and given the amount of debt (especially education related) and lack of savings in this country you have an obligation to sell more. The average American has only 3x their salary from life insurance coverage. I hope they don't plan on staying dead very long, because that money will run out quickly.

Go sell more term insurance.

Permanent Insurance:

Permanent or whole life insurance is guaranteed to be around for the whole life, hence the name. Unlike term insurance that runs out at some point, permanent insurance is there as long as your clients are.

Permanent insurance costs a lot more than term for the same amount of death benefit coverage. Like 5-15 times depending on how it is structured. But typically the prices are level (term generally increases in cost over time, because more 45 year olds die than 25 year olds. That is simply actuarial science.) and there is what is called the "interpolated terminal reserve" or "cash value", which is an asset designed to levelize the cost of the policy and allow a stoppage of premiums eventually.

This cash value is currently tax free growth under Section 7702 of the Internal Revenue Code through special named exclusions in subsections 101 (a) and (j). This is legalese/accountant speak to say that **the government endorses life insurance** by giving it special tax treatment. After tax dollars going in, no taxes on the growth, and as long as you follow the rules you can get the majority of the cash out tax free too. Similar to a ROTH IRA in many ways, without the income cap or annual limitations. Joe literally had a client with over $20million in cash value, growing completely and totally tax free.

Also cash value is currently not reportable as an asset on a financial aid form (FAFSA). 529's are brutalized and even parental retirement assets are included to some extent. Many benefits to cash value life insurance beyond the death benefit and tax shielded growth.

Think of cash value life insurance as the Swiss Army knife of financial products. There are better pure accumulation tools, better tax shields, things with more short term flexibility. But when you combine all of the benefits and applications, cash value life insurance can turn you as the planner into your client's financial MacGuyver. And isn't that ultimately what they want from you?

How Much Insurance is "Enough"?

Ok, we are going to blow your perception of reality up here. Because you have probably been taught about insurance all wrong.

Insurance of all forms (life insurance, home owners' insurance, disability coverage) replaces an asset in case of a loss. That asset could be your 3500-square foot home, or it could be the income stream from your client going to work every day.

Just like your client would be upset and probably sue if their car insurance only bought them a new bumper if their new Mercedes were totaled, or if their 3500-square foot mansion was replaced with a 900 square foot shed, if their family is living on $15,000 a month after tax income and you only sell them $2mm of coverage their family will be livid. Because that $2mm is a nice lump sum but will only generate about $4k a month adjusted for taxes and inflation as an income stream.

Given the ultra-low interest rate environment and the longevity of people, you can only count on 2-2.5% net after taxes and inflation for income for your clients. Think about that.

You were probably taught that 10x salary is a good amount of life insurance. Too few own even that mount. At that level only about

1/3 of the income is replaced. This only makes sense for a young married couple without kids to plan for as there is enough flexibility in the situation for the survivor to alter their lifestyle and time for them to recover emotionally. But if there are multiple children, a home that is part of the stability of their environment, and debt (mortgage, consumer debt, probably still student loans) and college down the road, more coverage is needed.

Joe uses 2.4% annual dispersal rate as a rule of thumb for clients (.2% per month) and would walk them through the derivation of that number. This is in the Model chapter. Once the client understands this, you can then help them calculate what coverage range makes sense for them. This is much more powerful than you spitting a number out of a computer, and the client is much more likely to purchase the coverage their family needs if you do so. Think about that for a moment.

So your client's family is really going to need almost 40x their income for their family to maintain the lifestyle they have built. A family living on $10k a month after taxes (probably $15k gross income) is going to need $10k/.024 = $4.17mm in insurance assuming no other assets or income.

College is extra. Like a new baby will need close to a million bucks to cover a private university, or a quarter million for a State school.

It takes on average $233,000 to raise a kid from birth to age 18 according to the latest data.

These numbers may blow your mind, but think about it for a moment as a cold calculation. Insurance is a replacement for the income stream. Savings for retirement drop when one of the partners die, and expenses are not proportionately reduced. In fact they often go up as the survivor takes on additional day care costs and changes tax status. Plus with the loss of a parent, the survivor tries to make up for it with more memories (like the Disney trip) and stuff, increasing the costs. Making life as "normal" as possible for the surviving spouse and kids means that you must essentially create an endowment that can withstand the market cycles and generate income while hedging for inflation. It is just math. In a low interest rate environment, you need more capital to create the same income stream. And we are close to the lowest interest rates ever, combined with longest potential lifespans so we need more for a longer period.

Top 5 Reasons to NOT Buy Permanent Insurance

Disclaimer: we own permanent insurance. And Joe has sold it. Lots of it. But only if it made sense for the client as part of their overall strategy. And Joe always received more questions on this basic strategy and tool than all the more complex parts of a plan combined. Seriously, someone would have no problem giving him a million dollars to manage, or putting together a trust or pay an attorney $8k for legal documents, but a $3,000 premium for a second to die policy to cover the estate taxes could illicit an hour-long discussion. So, to help clarify when this component makes sense, let's look to see the situations when it does not fit into a client's portfolio. None of these in and of itself is a knockout criteria, but if there are more than one then permanent insurance really probably is not an appropriate thing for your client to own.

1. **Don't owe anyone/don't care**. If there are no debts to cover, and no one financially dependent upon the client, then there is no insurable need. Pretty simple. Remember that people do fall in love and have kids, and that charitable support of an organization does create a dependency situation, so the leveraging potential of the death benefit to continue this support does make sense. But if your client is not worried about taking care of or helping anyone else, now or ever, then insurance is generally not an appropriate use of money.

2. **Not young and healthy**. The tax leverage of life insurance is generated by the internal tax free build up

and income tax free death benefit, both of which are paid for via the internal insurance charges. These charges are mainly driven by age and health, so if your clients are of advanced age or poor health, the costs of these components may overwhelm any tax advantages and disqualify permanent life insurance as a tool. If the plan however is to ultimately use the death benefit then even at advanced ages this can make sense as a leveraging tool.

3. **No tax need**. Many high-income individuals and corporations use the cash value as an accumulation tool since the internal cash grows tax free until touched and then may be accessed tax free. Academic analysis by Murtagh has shown that banks gain an extra 200+ basis points to their shareholders' return via BOLI (Bank Owned Life Insurance, a highly regulated and lucrative space. Essentially every bank uses BOLI because it is the most effective way to cover employee benefits and increase returns within the regulatory constraints.) Individuals in low tax brackets that can reasonably expect to not have income tax issues may not need the tax-free build-up of the policy as they have multiple other alternatives that may make more sense (such as Roth IRA's). But the clients you are talking with will almost all have a need for tax advantaged planning.

4. **Not enough time**. Permanent insurance is sometimes called "whole life insurance" because it is designed to cover that time: the whole entire lifetime. In reality, anything over 20 years really qualifies as an acceptable amount of time to allow the policy's acquisition charges to be amortized and the tax free build up to work. Calculations of the "buy term and invest the difference" model, assuming bond proxy rates of 4%-6%, generally show the superiority of the cash value insurance approach over extended periods. But if you are covering a need of five or ten years (e.g. a business loan, college tuitions for a high school student, etc) then term insurance is the

appropriate insurance coverage as it is designed for short term needs. Aligning coverage to time horizons like this is critical. If your clients are in their 20-50's time is on your side, if you are in your 70's probably not so.

5.   **Not enough money**. This is the main reason to gravitate towards term insurance over permanent coverage. If the calculations show that the individual needs $2.5 million of death benefit to do what they want if they are no longer around, Joe would have them buy that amount of coverage. Doing it as permanent insurance could be prohibitively expensive. Instead of taking the route of the less ethical insurance agents and settling for a quarter million of higher commission permanent coverage, a true professional like Templin would make sure the client gets the full amount of death benefit to protect their wishes even if it is not the optimal long range solution or yields the agent significantly less money. It is the right thing to do.

This is not an all-inclusive list of reasons to not use permanent insurance when it makes sense, but these five points cover the vast majority of the logical arguments against its use. We can actually prove using the Muller-Templin Simplification Ratio (in Models) from a mathematical basis that on an after tax, risk adjusted basis cash value life insurance is the most efficient wealth accumulation tool available, but the advanced mathematics is useless if you have a fundamental disagreement over whether or not Life Insurance makes sense.

The Case for Term Coverage

If the numbers show your client needs an additional $4.25mm of coverage for their spouse to stay in their home and the kids still do their activities and the college to be partially paid for like your client wants, don't be the selfish asshole that sells $250k of permanent coverage and collects the nice $3,000 paycheck. Because you are being money grubbing, commission driven self-centered asshole and an order taker, NOT a financial planner. That spouse should sue you if anything happens for dereliction of duty and fiduciary breach, because they trusted you as a professional to take care of their family if anything happened and you failed miserably at your job.

When Joe was a relatively new Rep there was an agent (also relatively new) that was held up as a shining example to the others at an annual office meeting. This guy had hardcore sold his brother to get him to buy life insurance, to protect his wife and two little girls. This is in the late 90's and the guy made $100k a year in Upstate NY, so pretty good money. And his brother got him to do the right thing. OR so it seemed.

The Rep had sold his brother $300k of permanent coverage. And then the brother died. Three hundred thousand of insurance to replace his income and pay for two Sweet 16's and college and all that. $300k was barely enough to cover the mortgage. The brother that was held up as a paragon of virtue screwed his brother and his nieces and his sister in law because it was easier to go into sales mode on a sexy accumulation oriented insurance product (and make $5k) than it was to really do the right thing and sell his brother two million of term insurance with a hundred thousand of permanent coverage as a base and then exchange some of the term coverage for permanent coverage each year.

He was a self-centered lazy ass who took the easy route and his nieces will pay the price for their entire lives. Their mom had to enter the workforce a few years later after a decade of not working. What stress did that add? She had to pull the girls from certain programs. Think they were happy giving up these friendships and experiences?

This is a case where term insurance would be the right thing. Whenever you have a large need and limited cash flow to address it, term insurance is the tool. Just like permanent coverage it is neither good nor bad, it merely is appropriate or inappropriate. Term will get the job done for the client if anything happens short term, and buy time to adjust the planning as situations change.

Annuities: Unless your clients work for a governmental entity (military, teacher, insurance department, etc.) they probably will not have a pension when they retire. Yet with the dramatically increasing lifespans of the past three generations (from low sixties to roughly eighty today), the need to have income that cannot be outlived is becoming more and more in demand with clients.

And not just the Baby Boomer knocking on the door of retirement: a recent report indicated that the Millennial Generation is overwhelmingly in favor of having guaranteed income for the long range and is willing to pay for it. Annuities are the perfect vehicle for this. Regular boring annuities (either fixed or variable) do not require any medical underwriting and carry some excellent privileges that make them highly useful in certain situations, such as:

1. A client leaving an employer with a pension plan (or employer terminates the plan) can usually roll out the pension into an annuity, which still gives them the guaranteed income stream they had been promised. Using a variable annuity for a client that is not going to retire for at least a decade and a half will almost always create more income in retirement for them than leaving it with the employer, while giving them superior distribution options.

2. A variable annuity will not only provide income in retirement, but could provide an inflation hedge over time. If your client is expecting to live over two decades in retirement, do you think that inflation might become a concern for them over time?

3. Many annuities will lock in your client's mortality based on current tables. That means that if they turn the annuity into an income stream in twenty or thirty years, they will receive checks probably 20% bigger than they would if they waited to purchase the annuity just

because of the mortality differences. Do you think your client would want more or less money in retirement?

4. Due to the mortality credits built in, an annuity allows someone to generate the income they need with guarantees for about 1/3 less capital. So that client that only has $600K can shave more income than one with $800k.

5. The popular press rails against the fees of variable annuities, but some of the better ones have fees close to that of the average mutual fund. So you can help the client diversify their portfolio, guarantee the future income, have tax advantages, and still be cost competitive.

6. Did we mention that most variable annuities have a wide selection of investments, so that you can build a fully diversified portfolio, often with lower asset sizes? And that you can schedule automatic re-balancing of the portfolio, to make sure that the asset allocation remains where your client wants it to be, with no additional time from you?

7. Also, if this is non-tax shielded money (i.e. not IRA or Roth), the annuity creates tax deferral which ultimately creates more money (and income) for your client? And the re-balancing would be a non-taxable event too!

8. Fixed annuities do not have the upside potential of a variable annuity, but given the current economic conditions many clients are seeking guaranteed returns above that of their savings accounts. One percent taxable versus two plus percent tax deferred, which would you rather have?

Why aren't you recommending it to some of your clients? Is it "Waaaahh, it's too hard!"? Or is it "But they heard Suze Orman say bad things about them!" BUNK! You are the professional, not the client. And you know your client's situation, not the pretty teeth on TV that is compensated to draw eyeballs instead of solve problems like you are. You have a moral obligation (and maybe even a legal one) to make sure the clients are ok in retirement, which includes making sure they don't run out of cash.

There are numerous other uses of annuities that we do not really have the time to delve into, but there already exist a vast variety of resources in the industry for you to look to with help in application of the concepts. One of the single best books on this is Tom Hegna's "Paychecks and Playchecks" (www.tomhegna.com), which draws on thousands of hours of academic research. We HIGHLY recommend you read it, if you want to actually understand annuities and make money using them to help your clients.

Just remember that annuities in the right place can be of tremendous help to your clients and to your business.

Long Term Care: The fastest growing demographic in the United States by percentage is those over 100 years old, followed by those over 85 years old. Followed by those 65 and greater. Do you notice a trend?

America is graying very quickly, partially because of the longevity issues that we discussed above concerning annuities. And medical science is one of the major drivers. One hundred years ago no one knew what Alzheimer's Disease was. Now everybody not even knows what it is but probably has some experience with a loved one having it, and needing extra attention because they ca not take care of themselves. Fifty years ago a heart attack was almost certain death. Now people have multiple heart attacks because they can survive the first and even second thanks to 911 and better treatment in the hospital and after the fact. Same with strokes. Accidents that snap people's necks twenty years ago would have caused death. Now they "just" disable people. Some quadriplegics actually recover and can lead something approaching normal lives, but most don't and require round the clock care that can last years or decades.

There are more people in need of constant care in the US now than there were people in the country at our founding.

Long Term Care Insurance offsets these costs, creating revenue that can pay caregivers (including family and friends), facilities, and other expenses. It can keep an elderly person in their own home so that they maintain their dignity, it can help a young person heal and relearn how to live. It will prevent family feuds over who is going to take in grandma, and it will protect investment portfolios and college savings that would otherwise be pillaged to cover these costs.

Long Term Care is a smart investment by a client because it will make sure that the spouse that does not go into a retirement home can stay in their own home instead of going bankrupt. It can protect the family legacy. Long Term Care enjoys all sorts of tax advantages on the federal and state level because it ultimately will save the country money by shifting the risk to the insurance companies that can handle it. What other product do you sell where the government will pay your client to buy it?

Group Benefits: Even with Obamacare there are some opportunities. There is more in force group disability coverage in the US than there is individual coverage, and on the life insurance side it is close. Plus there are those retirement plans that you might want to be managing.

Joe had a very nice group benefits business that he built via referral to another organization. His primary company owned a group benefits firm that Joe would introduce the appropriate clients (HR Directors, Presidents, etc.) to and literally get out of the way, letting the experts in this area do the work while he collected a portion of the revenues. Yes, Joe gave up 60% of the cash-flow but gave up 100% of the work, creating the most profitable component of his business on a per hour of effort basis. You can do the exact same thing, and we would recommend that you do so.

Every time the company hires a new employee, they enroll in the group benefits plan and you get a raise. Fast growing companies produce large jumps in monthly revenue for you. By having the group coverage you also get the opportunity to do the individual planning, so you can be paid multiple times on the same relationship.

Group benefits includes group life or disability coverage, health and dental insurance, retirement benefits, as well as some non-traditional benefits like pre-paid services (legal, accounting, etc.) and educational planning. Many property and casualty companies have other benefits that make sense in this space too. Double check with your firm as to what you offer and what you are allowed to broker or refer out, as this can be a very lucrative division of your business if you are allowed to participate in it.

There are numerous studies discussing the importance of cross selling for the health and longevity of your business, and we can tell you anecdotally that clients prefer the situation of one planner executing the majority of the financial plan as opposed to having stuff all over the place. Happier clients giving you more money and introductions is not a bad thing, and cross selling is the best way to achieve this.

So in the end, why should you have multiple products that you sell? There is always the old adage that you can't build a house with just a hammer, which is completely true.

Also, if a client rejects buying investments from you they may buy the Disability Insurance or Long Term Care Insurance, and then as their situation changes they could come around and purchase the life coverage and investments, which happens more frequently than you might think.

We have a friend that is a firefighter. As he says, if you can't get in through the door there are the windows. And if John is assigned a target, he will use whatever tool he needs to accomplish his mission.

Think about this for a moment as it applies to your business as a Financial Advisor and cross selling other products to help your clients.

SOP's

If you were military you would instantly recognize that an SOP is a Standard Operating Procedure. Dictionary.com does not have an actual definition for this, so let's just go with "The way we do things, every time, so we get predictable results."

McDonald's brought SOP's to the restaurant business. Say what you will, but they have served billions and billions and become the most valuable company in their space by having a consistent process (taught at Hamburger U). Every franchise does everything exactly the same from defrosting the burgers to cooking fries to how they are supposed to fill out a timecard. Think about it: the assembly line concept that Henry Ford used to change the landscape of America (both physical and business) extended to another industry and tremendous wealth created. What if you were to extend these concepts into your financial planning business?

Well, Joe did with John's assistance. He was able to leave the office every single day around 5:00 to either go to Tae Kwon Do or have dinner. Joe was able to reduce his stress levels because he had SOP's for everything within his office, and his clients had total confidence in him and his staff (THANK YOU Tara Beaugy!!!). And he was able to keep over FIVE appointments per day on average between his production and management responsibilities. The office was a well-oiled machine. Would you like to replicate this?

Instead of trying to create procedures from scratch, first look to see what you can steal. We mean adopt from others.

Does your compliance department have a checklist of paperwork you need for each type of account? Steal it.

Does your primary insurance carrier have a process for paperwork and underwriting? STEAL IT!

Maybe SOP should really mean "Stole Other People's Processes", because if they work you should steal/borrow/adopt them and tweak as appropriate for your needs. Using 90% of other's development work is an efficient way to build your work flows so that you can ramp up quickly.

So we are going to give you some of the SOP's and processes that we have developed specifically for the financial services world. Adopt and modify them as you see appropriate, because this is one of the secrets to transitioning into a continuous growth stage of your business.

We will not give you an SOP for every single aspect of your business because your business is none of our business. But hopefully we give you enough to make a difference, and for you to build off of. Understanding your own needs and having the skill set to start addressing them is critical to your development as a business owner, and our giving you just a little instead of everything is tough love as it will make you think and grow.

Appointment Confirmation SOP

The importance of the Confirmation SOP cannot be overstated, because it will increase your percentage of appointments kept by up to 25%. Meaning you can have a huge jump in productivity and feel better that people aren't blowing you off nearly as often, which can be soul sucking.

1. **Scheduled.** When you schedule the appointment (or your team does), end the conversation with "And if you cannot make the appointment for some reason, please give us the professional courtesy of two days' notice so that we can slide someone else into that spot. Just like you would let your attorney, accountant, or doctor know if you need to

reschedule." This puts you on par with those professionals and makes the client realize you are busy, i. e. successful.

2. **Email.** Same day that the appointment is scheduled, the client needs to get an email (and preferably calendar invite) that has your contact info and the details of the appointment. If you have any additional info (like your professional bio or info on the firm) that is background this should be included.

3. **Two business days in advance.** Client should get a call from your office reminding them of the appointment. NB: do NOT call to confirm your own appointment. Makes you look small time. Joe as a new Rep shared an office with another guy (Jeremy Berry, CPA turned financial advisor and a heck of a guy) and they would confirm each other's appointments to give the image of success. Because a client will try to weasel out with you, but not with a staff member.

4. **Meeting.** Clients can never leave the meeting without the next one scheduled. Even if it is only penciled in because they have to confirm with their significant other. Joe's clients would walk out of his office and Tara would schedule the appointment, and the clients would see on her screen that he was 70% booked for the next two weeks and thus that appointment slot was important! **Scarcity creates desire.**

5. **Follow Up.** Every client after every meeting would get a summary and action items from Joe. Even if it was saying no further action at this point. This letter was a good CYA but also would make sure that the client was moving long wherever they were in the process of financial planning.

So five contacts from Joe's office for every meeting. Might seem redundant, but he kept 70%+ of his appointments. And almost all clients came to his office or they were teleconferences. This process works. It also contributes to the Reliability component of the Trust Factor. Think about that.

Agendas

We would use an agenda for every single meeting. It makes you look more professional, it lets the client know exactly what you intend to cover (you can add things that they want to discuss btw), it protects the integrity of your process, it gets you more introductions, and it makes good cover for the inevitable lawsuit.

You will be sued eventually. It is the nature of our business and Society as a whole. So CYA. Document everything. Make sure Compliance signs off on everything the need to. If you follow SOP's, document everything, and act ethically you really have nothing to worry about.

Always make two copies of your agendas. One is for your files, the other is for your client to keep. If you are face to face with the client, have them initial your copy so that ten years from now you can produce it and show that you did review that portfolio before the market melted down and recommended they change allocations.

If you are not meeting them face to face, make sure the agenda is emailed to them with return receipt requested. Does the same thing as having client initial.

So here are the agendas that Joe would use for an initial Fact Finding meeting and his presentation meeting. Feel free to steal.

AGENDA: FIRST MEETING

1. **Introductions**

2. **Overview of Process**

3. **Mutual Expectations**

4. **Information Gathering**

   a. **Facts**

       b. **Feelings**

       c. **Philosophies**

   5. **Clarification of Goals and Objectives**

   6. **Red Flags**

   7. **Favorable Introductions**

   8. **Next Appointment:**

Expected Time of Meeting: 90 minutes.

AGENDA: PRESENTATION MEETING

   1. **Review of Goals and Objectives**

   2. **Review of Analysis**

   3. **Recommendations**

   4. **Implementation Decision:**

       a. **Yes**

       b. **No**

       c. **Need Additional Information:**

   5. **Execution Steps**

   6. **Favorable Introductions**

   7. **Next Appointment:**

Expected Time of Meeting: 90 minutes.

Don't forget having an agenda for your reviews with clients. Great time for introductions, term insurance conversions, and increasing contributions to Roths/529s.

Feeder Lists:

Every meeting Joe would have a feeder list of potential Introductions from the client. To make it easy for the client, Joe would invest the five minutes of pre-work via cyber-stalking and be ready to present the list. There was a reason he averaged over five introductions on initial meetings and three on second meeting, two plus on every review meeting.

So here is a prototypical feeder list drawn from a client's Linkedin connections. Names have been changed to protect the guilty.

Introductions Desired from J. Tolkein

Frodo Baggins: Guardian Regional Director (Bree)

Lyle Buryniak: AHL CDO (The Shire)

Corey Squire: Southwest Mortgage of Louisiana

Rosanne Lieutenant: VP HR Grubb Insurance

Frank Legolas: NML MD, Mirkwood Advisors

Craig Septlan: NML CDO, San Francisco

Rob Cherry: CDO BBL, NYC

Francisco Salsa: Director of Development, IML, NYC

Sauron DeWhite: RVP, RIMutual

Orc "Raiding" Party, VP at Slash Brokerage

Italics represent previous relationship with JRRT

Bold indicates strongly desired introduction

We aren't going to explain the reasoning behind the dark or italics. We want you to struggle and figure out the WHY behind these, so that you understand and believe more. The art of the poet is to not say everything.

Presentations:

Joe had a template for single people, married couples/partners without kids, married/partnered with dependent kids, married/partnered with grown kids. This allowed him to shorten input times for analysis, the presentations printed the exact same pages for each type of presentation (in proper order), and he knew his presentation pages inside out and backwards/forwards from practice. More efficient. What templates for presentations make sense for your business?

Remember: anything that you have to do more than once a year in your business really should have a Standard Operating Procedure associated with it to save time and ensure consistency. We have given you these SOP's (plus the Language which is an SOP when you think about it) as these are the areas we have discovered will have almost the greatest impact on your business.

There is only one other area that SOP's are overlooked and need to be applied as it will radically improve your business: calendaring.

Most (especially new) financial advisors meet with clients whenever the client wants to meet, because they value that meeting more than they value themselves.

Stop it.

Control your calendar.

You will be more efficient.

You will see more people.

You will have less stress.

You will be more professional.

Your staff and family won't want to kill you.

You'll make more money.

Now, a word on your ideal calendar. It is an ideal, like a massless frictionless pulley with a massless frictionless string with zero stretch in your basic physics class. You will rarely run your ideal calendar (but when you do it feels awesome). But if you can come close the majority of the time you are doing a great job. Only machines and David Hilton Jr. are perfect at this.

Joe's Ideal Calendar:

Bed Night Before:	10:30
Wake Up:	4:40
Drive to Gym:	4:45
Workout:	5:00
Shower/Dress:	6:30
Prep/Focus/Practice:	6:45
Appointment 1:	7:00
Staff Meeting:	8:30
Phoning:	9:00

Management Meeting:	9:15
Appointment 2:	10:00
Appointment 3:	11:30
Appointment 4:	1:00
Appointment 5:	2:30
Appointment 6:	4:00
Paperwork/stuff:	5:00
Leave Office:	5:10
Tae Kwon Do or Dinner:	5:30
Review of Day:	8:30
Study Time:	9:00
Self Time:	10:00

Notice how we start our ideal day the night before. If you are out partying like a rock star until four am, you are not getting up and working out and having an early start. That simple.

Early in his career Joe only did Tae Kwon Do 2-3 nights a week, and the other nights he would have appointments at 5:30 and 7:00. He earned the right to do Tae Kwon Do or have dinner with family/friends (often clients!) instead of working evenings because he didn't goof off during the day.

If an appointment canceled Joe would do the things that needed to be done like follow up with clients, additional phoning, case review, etc.

Joe would have 2 lunches a day, his 11:30 and 1:00 meetings. He almost never met someone for lunch at noon because it was inefficient. He would also have lunch delivered to the office instead of going to a restaurant most of the time because he could totally control the environment.

If a client had rescheduled with two days' notice (as almost all did, because Joe and his staff had told them to), then that spot would usually be filled by another client that wanted to see Joe or management/recruiting/development meetings. There is a reason Joe kept over 5 appointments a day ON AVERAGE for over a decade. You can approach this by using these SOP's.

Essentially all of Joe's meetings were in his office or teleconference. Don't have to worry about weather, or parking, or traffic. More efficient, and if a client was a few minutes late Joe could fill out that trade or review a case file or return a client call in those tiny cracks of time that you are probably wasting.

If Joe had to go see a client at their office, he would schedule at least three meetings in the same building to maximize time. Once he literally scheduled 22 appointments (one hour meetings) over two days in the same office. He kept 95 meetings that month, with a week off for Christmas. Think about how you can do this…

Control your calendar if you want to increase your production tremendously. Or not. This is a choice that you need to make. Chose wisely. Chose to use Standard Operating Procedures so that your systems run your business instead of your business running you.

It's a Trap!

Yes, you read that in Admiral Akbar's voice. And if we did not re-direct you now, your head would be filling with internet memes of Akbar declaring "It's a trap!" layered over pictures of decaf coffee or cute fluffy kittens with machine guns. Go ahead, try to purge them from your mind. Try to not think of a STOP sign.

You thought of a STOP sign, didn't you? Of course you probably did, because the vast majority of people would because we set you up to do so. The question is, are you setting up STOP signs and traps for yourself? Probably, because of some bad programming in your wetworks between the ears.

Would you like to override some of that programming?

Would you like to recognize some of the patterns that lead to failure and negativity, before you go too far down that neural pathway and get caught?

If you were to think about it for a moment, the answer would probably be YES. And partially because we are using the ideas behind the traps you've set for yourself to give you the illusion of choice in the matter of breaking the patterns of failure. We are tricking you into succeeding mentally even as you read this sentence. And it will be all the more powerful because you think it is your idea. You might want to re-read the previous couple of sentences and think about that, and how to apply it in your business.

We recognize that traps of a physical nature are not nearly as dangerous for you as they would be for say Dr. Stolk in his old line of work that included going into bad places after bad people that want to do bad things. We doubt you have to deal with trip wires or incoming fire. You do not face bodily harm and death regularly in your financial services career as it is rare for someone to even threaten to physically throw you out. But the psychological dangers are very real and insidious. If you absorb what we present in this chapter, your awareness of these threats will dramatically increase.

Once again we decided to present this section in a vignette style so that once you read it once, you can pick and choose which parts are most relevant to you at any given time in helping you make your choices to create a financial services career.

Laing's Model: A Psychotic World

One thing about psychiatrists is that they are not immune to mental illness, and a shining example of this was Scottish shrink R. D. Laing whose son declared "My father solved other people's problems, but not his own." We are not perfect and have our own issues, but we can objectively look at external situations and help you assess and understand them. Like how the world is really a giant psychotic episode.

To give you a quick overview one needs to understand what Laing (and we) refer to as the Two Selves.

There is the public presentation of whom we are, which is full of illusion and some bluster. We try to put on our best appearance (ever hear "fake it 'til you make it" in training?). It is the Doctor (or financial adviser) in debt up to their eyeballs yet driving the new flashy car. It is the soccer mom with the perfect Christmas picture that is at all the recitals and drinking a bottle of wine a night after the kids are in bed. Cobbler's kid with no shoes, or attorney without a will and estate plan. It is the forced white shirt and boring tie in the office so as to fit in with the culture. In financial services it is the illusion of success because "successful people want to work with other successful people." It is the pretty surface that once scratched reveals a not so pretty situation beneath.

As an engineer will tell you, if the foundation to the building is not strong and crack free, you will have issues later. If you think for a moment, psychologically this is the same situation. People build big flashy houses adorned with trappings of success on shifting sands. Not super stable.

Think about how often you've been told "fit in", "don't make waves", "polish yourself". There are hundreds of phrases that you have heard thousands of time telling you to be something other than who you really are "because it's better for you". To be like all the sheeple that have the face they show the public and a very different one known only to them and maybe those closest to them. This public face is what Laing calls the "False Self". It is a cocoon of half-truths and lies of various shades of white and grey that covers the true being within.

Hidden within this False Self is the True Self. This is what we admit to ourselves and those closest to us. This is where we admit that we like watching Spongebob Squarepants, or that we hate doing Thanksgiving with the in-laws. This is where our edge is, the things that are not fully socially acceptable yet invigorate us. This is the kernel of terror of being poor again like when we grew up and were embarrassed, or that fear of celery that one of Joe's close friends has and only a few know about. The constant need to prove ourselves because we have doubt. It is all the weird things outside of the "normal" distribution that when aggregated really make us unique and stick out instead of blending in the way our educational system is designed to do.

If you know anyone that is absolutely world class in something, they are probably "a little off". It is partially why they are so good. Joe is a dork, and those who meet him know this. He was most powerful and effective as a financial planner when he embraced his dorkiness (with an edge) instead of trying to fit in or please others. The True Self is where power resides. "Know Thyself."

Note we are not talking being a weirdo for the sake of being a weirdo, nor are we talking about trying to be different (like all the people you know with similar tattoos that are meant to show how individualistic they are) for the sake of getting attention. Not a hipsteresque embracing of something like artisanal pickles. One of those things that when you discover it about a friend you say "OK, that's weird. I don't get it, tell me more." It is a core that is out of sync with the accepted mores of family and our Society, and remains even as the world and trappings change.

The True Self is the reason why little kids tell the truth even when it can be embarrassing to the big people around. It is why the grumpy old lady says what she thinks without giving a damn what you or the rest of the people think. It is partially why Donald Trump beat Hillary Clinton, because even many of the ardent Democrats KNEW and admitted she was untrustworthy. Trump was like the drunk uncle: you didn't agree with everything but you resonated with parts of what he said, whether it was talking about Washington corruption or the raw deal Sanders got in the primary or the mess that was the foreign policy and multiple undeclared wars or the disconnect between Washington and the rest of the country. And quite frankly those in the middle economically were fed up with the disconnect of the elites and were desperate to change the direction the country was going.

There is the old saying "In wine there is truth" because alcohol can strip away some of the False Self. It reveals some of the "don't give a fu(<" and resonates, making people want to say "Hell yeah!" and "Amen!". In an insane world, crazy is truth.

The friction between the True Self and False Self is one of the reasons why we see successful people implode and a higher degree of harmful actions (alcoholism, divorce, excessive risk taking, etc.) in financial services because of the extreme cultures of "our way", the white shirt with dark suit and boring tie way our field has evolved over the past hundred years. It also partly explains the low closing rates and high failure rates of new recruits to the financial services profession.

Per Laing we are living a gigantic psychotic episode as False Selves interact with each other. All of the sales processes designed to "build rapport" are nothing more than two liars discussing their lies and agreeing to accept them from each other. That's why getting a 25% closing rate is the goal of most sales programs, because liars lying to each other can rarely agree on truth and develop trust.

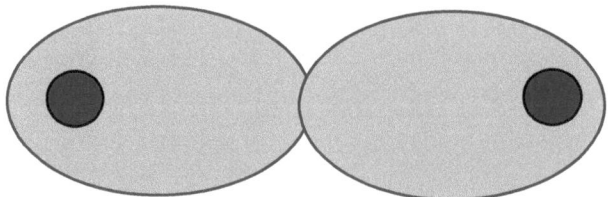

Now imagine if you had little or no False Self. Furthermore, understand that there are ways to reduce and eliminate the False Self illusion from your potential client while you are talking to them. True Self, communicating with True Self. How often does that really happen?

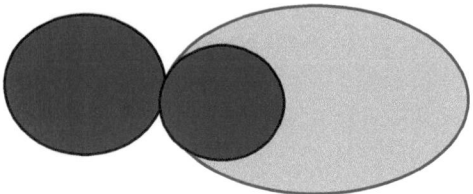

When you can do this, your closing rates will jump to 50% and even higher, because Truth is powerful and rare. DO not fall for the trap of the illusion of self.

For more information on The Divided Self, go to http://laingsociety.org/biblio/divself.htm

Two Planner Trap

Joe had a client who had been with him since he was 21 years old and one of the first hires for a tech company. Fast forward about a decade and the company gets sold and he gets a large payday. All of the sudden other financial and investment advisors were coming out of the woodwork.

Normally wouldn't bother Joe at all because his clients knew what he had done for them with the total planning, both financial and beyond. Review "Association" in the Trust Factor as to why this should have been a non-issue. And Joe had a rule: you were either my client, or you weren't. Within six months of becoming his "client" you had to implement all of the basic strategies he had recommended (basic legal stuff, insurances, fixing beneficiaries, etc.) and he had to manage the investments where possible (work related things he couldn't, nor other trusts and the like). Or you weren't his client. In or out. Trust and work with Joe, or don't.

Why? Because he wasn't having someone else be paid for the planning work he did. If you were to think about that for a minute, you would now have to conclude that that is fair. And you would want the same thing we guess.

Secondly, he didn't want to have only part of the portfolio and be compared against another advisor because they could get lucky in the market or chose the hot idea that lasts for another six months but ignore the taxes or allocations or risk and ultimately end up harming the client financially.

Third, the client deals with two different philosophies. Either your clients fully believe in you and your approach, or they don't. No halfway commitments, because they would end up like the squirrel that half way committed to running across the road. SQUISH! Just like grape to quote Mr. Miyagi.

When Joe's client got the big payout from the sale of the business, suddenly that client's father's planner, who had no time for him when he was 21 and had no money, wanted in and Dad gave son a bunch of heat. A LOT of pressure. Like remove from the will type pressure.

Joe didn't get to manage any of the new assets, and the other guy kept switching up what he was doing so Joe couldn't even hedge what was going on because he had no clue what his other guy was up to (We hate having "the other guy". It's worse than having "the other person" in a relationship with a cheater. At least then someone is getting screwed in a good way. Think about that.)

The results are as predictable as you can expect, especially when the market was down or sideways and the other guy was trying to make a splash.

One plan, one planner. Not a bunch of people competing like on the Bachelorette. Either you do the work or not, because you should not emotionally and businessly invest yourself in a client and not be able to do the right thing and have them get hurt by another planner that doesn't play nicely.

This is not to say you can't have a pair of planners working for the client together IN HARMONY. Stolk and Templin often work with clients together with other professionals, often with some overlap of skill sets. Multiple doctors of different disciplines creating

78

coordinated care is a good idea, same with attorneys of different specialties. If you are working together, discussing the strategies, communicating regularly so there is ONE plan for your client that is totally OK. But don't have multiple voices in their head, because it will make them financially crazy and you totally frustrated.

SMILE!

Dr. Stolk came across an interesting psychosomatic phenomenon. Along the lines of the old "fake it 'til you make it." Trick your body by smiling.

A relatively small study found that people with severe depression who were injected with Botox (yes, a deadly disease that is essentially watered down and shot in your face with a giant needle to paralyze the muscles and make you pretty. Think about THAT for a minute in relation to False Self and then weep for humanity's vanity!) so that they were unable to frown stopped frowning. OK, they couldn't frown because those muscles were temporarily paralyzed. And over the next week and month, since they couldn't frown the participants smiled a LOT more.

This lead to them reporting being happier at a very statistically significant rate. Keep in mind these people had been on significant medication, in counselling and therapy, and many had their lives essentially shut down from depression. And they reported greater results from this "anti-frown" experiment than any other treatment. Think about that.

Now remind yourself to smile. Get a mirror and smile in it before you do your dialing, or go into an appointment.

Set an alarm on your phone eight times a day, to smile.

Watch a funny kid.

Sign up for a joke of the day website.

Get your daily does of Vitamin L: Laughter.

The medical support for increased immune system, lower stress levels, and higher productivity are numerous from laughing a few times a day. Studies also show greater creativity and increased sales production.

So make yourself smile and laugh even if you are not in the mood, because it will break your bad mood. And no one wants to buy product from a grump!

Commission Breath

Never figure out you are going to be paid on any particular case you are working on until after it is submitted at the earliest. Why?

Because when you realize that you will be paid over $15,000 if you can get this particular client to buy that particular product you are recommending, you become tainted. It is in your mind, subconsciously you lust after that payday and the client can sense it. Especially if you NEED to make the sale because you are running out of money.

The best way to avoid Commission Breath is to not give a damn about the payday you'll get from that trade or policy or product. One way to have this happen is never figure out what it is worth to you until after the client agrees, because then you can truthfully answer to the client if they do ask "ya know, I have no idea what I'd be paid if you do this. Doesn't matter to me, I am suggesting you do it because it is the right thing for YOU."

Another good way to avoid Commission Breath is to run a high activity business. If a particular IRA rollover you are trying to secure is worth $5,000 to you that could be a big deal if it is your one and only chance to make money this week because you have almost no appointments. But if later today you also have a rollover that will pay you $2k and a life insurance close worth $3k and a Long Term Care case worth $6k, and you have forty open cases you are working on worth potentially $90k of revenue in the next six weeks, no one particular case will make or break you.

Clients can sense if you are in need like a dog smells fear. So be not afraid.

Yes, if you have a career level case you are pitching that will pay you half a million dollars it is a big deal. So is taking the shot to win the championship. But if you convince yourself it is the same as a case that will pay you $500, that it is no big deal, that it is just another shot in the game, you will not tighten up and mess it up.

Relax and let it flow and do the right thing, because there is always another big deal if you are actually running hard in the business like a true professional. Don't fall for the Commission Breath trap.

The Champion Pose

One of the most iconic images from sports cinema is of Rocky Balboa at the top of the steps in Philadelphia, arms raised over his head in triumph. So important was this one scene that they actually put a statue at the top of the stairs in celebration of it. Not bad for a guy that was rejected dozens of times and had to sell his dog to survive. But we think Stallone is doing ok now financially.

The pose Rocky strikes at the top of the stairs (and the mountain in one of the later movies) is something that is innate, a celebration of victory. We have been striking that pose since before we were even human, as all of the great apes will assume the Champion Pose after a victory over another.

But here is the thing, like 13-year-old Cassius Clay who was already in his mind the Champion of the World: the pose should come first. Striking and holding the Champion Pose for two minutes will release a variety of hormones in your system that reduce stress and inflammation as well as increase pleasure.

A couple of minutes before going into a big meeting, hide in the bathroom stall or your office or the stairway, close your eyes, and raise your arms in victory over your head. Hold it for two minutes, feeling the power of victory flow through you. Your probability of getting the deal is over 25% greater than if you don't do it. That is a pretty darn good return on investment.

We will layout in depth reasons behind WHY this works and some studies in support of it at a later time. But as an anecdote, Joe tried this before each of the legs of a couple of his Ragnars in 2016. A Ragnar is a 200ish mile team relay race where each runner runs three separate legs for a total of 15-20 miles over a day to day and a half. It's nuts, and addictive if you are touched in the head in the right way.

So Joe struck Champion Pose before each of his legs (and during sometimes while running). His WORST performance was beating his projected time for that leg by 7%, best was over 15% better. Now this is completely unscientific in that there was no control group and a single subject with under a dozen data points, but the fact that it worked EVERY SINGLE TIME and costs absolutely nothing out of pocket would indicate that trying this trick, trapping yourself for success, might be a good idea.

Loss Leader

This Trap is a story related by Ryan Pinney, a Top of the Table Producer (that's well over a MILLION a year of gross commissionable premium. He does a TON of business each year and gives back to the profession through NAIFA and MDRT, and like Joe is a former 4 Under 40 Winner from Advisor Today):

I worked retail sales many years ago for a high-end audio/video retailer. We would routinely ask customers looking for a "loss-leader" product from an advertisement if they had a moment to check out our new latest, greatest TV, stereo, home theater, etc. we had just gotten in.

It was a set-up. A trap!

Using the "I would like your opinion or thoughts on..." as the lead in, we would hand them the remote, tell them what buttons to hit and paint the mental picture of what they were about to experience as they did so. It's pretty hard not to be amazed seeing/hearing a $30,40,50k home theater system or $10k/each speakers...which invariably leads the customer to ask "how much does this cost..." followed by a "that's way too much...".

We were taught to quickly grab the remote away from them with a comment along the lines of "well, let's go find something more in your price range..." 9/10 times the customer had forgotten the "loss-leader" they came in for and would decide that they wanted something nicer/more comparable to what they had been shown but in the top end of their price range - often 4-5x above the initial price of the advertised product.

This happens for a few reasons:

1. They see the value/capabilities/benefits of spending more on nicer/better equipment/products.
2. They have been challenged to find "their price range".
3. They have something to prove.

Think about how often you have fallen for this trap. Have you used it on clients?

THE SAG Factor

Engineers and the military love acronyms. Luckily they don't have to communicate with regular humans that often, so they can speak their own esoteric language and it doesn't matter that much. Financial services has tons of acronyms too, and unfortunately we slip into our jargon with clients way too often. Remember: if the client could speak the language they wouldn't need you. So speak English to them (or whatever language they speak).

Sometimes though you might want to use an acronym to stir interest in the client. Just like referring to "a 7702 plan" and discussing the aspects of it (after tax contribution and tax deferral just like a Roth, with a few caveats to get tax free distribution but no taxable income restrictions like those on a Roth. Plus guarantees on the principal well over the $250k the FDIC gives) to get them excited before finally telling them that 7702 refers to the section of the Internal Revenue Code that defines life insurance, you may want to indirectly talk about certain things via an acronym before bluntly hitting your clients with the meaning. Like with the SAG Factor.

SAG Factor is the single best model we have discovered for predicting long range failure after the first full year in the financial services profession.

SAG Factor also impacts clients. It will allow you to predict how much of an allocation of resources (staff time, your time, emotional reserves) they will use.

SAG Factor is multiplicative, so each factor in and of itself does not determine failure nor success. An average rating for each component is 10.00 with every standard deviation being an addition 2, and you should determine how far above or below average you are. And if you just said to yourself "oh, I'm well above average", give yourself a 14 for arrogance.

If you didn't instantly recognize that being above average is not a good thing, give yourself a 12 on S.

If you are only slightly above average on any of the three SAG factors you should assign yourself a 10.5-12.0 rating. The fact that you are in the financial services industry heralds scores in this range as a minimum on each factor as those who are below average in these areas tend to not even consider financial services, and with the current environment probably are not recruited.

So as an illustration, let's say you gave yourself a 11.5 on the one factor, and 12.00's on the other two. That would give you a SAG Factor of 11.5 x 12.0 x 12.0 yields 35.5.

OK, if you actually were doing the calculation you'd know that it is 1656, which is a big difference. If you didn't get 1656 you should raise your S score. Probably your A also as you jumped to the conclusion and didn't check your work.

So we should probably tell you the individual factors at this point as you are probably guessing and chomping at the bit because we withheld the information from you.

But first, let this be a lesson to you. If a client calculates the answer as opposed to you presenting it to them, they value it more. They won't doubt an answer the calculator or computer spits out that they input with your guidance nearly as much as they doubt an answer you give them. You can probably think of some applications of this in your business.

So the three components of SAG are Stupidity, Arrogance, and Greed. Does that bother you? Too bad. Science does not care who it offends, as it focuses on the truth. Maybe you should go back and review False Self/True Self.

Stupidity is actually the first one that will present itself. Maybe it is difficulty passing the licensing exams. Or it could be inability to understand how to read a financial statement or report. Whatever the case may be, remember that Financial Services is NOT nuclear engineering (Joe knows, he was a nukie), and he helped write some licensing exams and a ton of CE. You can actually overcome this risk, and as long as you are aware of it and understand your limits you can mitigate the risk fairly well.

If you lack high native intelligence you can always make up for it by working hard. And understanding that you are not the most brilliant person in the room will help keep your A score in check.

The second two factors are much bigger threats to long range success whereas S is more of a short-term issue because if you totally lack the brain power to pass exams and meet the minimal thresholds in our industry, you won't make it past initial six months we referenced that SAG applies to. In fact excessive scores on either A or G could lead to disaster if high enough, as we saw with ENRON and NOKIA and multiple other organizations. You can also use these to predict with high certainty if an individual client will be a pain in the keister long range too.

A is Arrogance as you have probably surmised. Pride goeth before the fall to quote the old adage. Arrogance leads to under-respecting your adversaries, the competition, and the markets. It leads to believing you are above the law and leads to excessive risk taking. When fueled by large quantities of money, Arrogance is exceedingly dangerous to long range success.

Remember there is a difference between Arrogance and Confidence. Some of the most powerful people we know are humbly confident.

Greed is NOT good, no matter what Gordon Gecko claimed. It is a driver of failure. It is also inversely related to the SO score in the Trust Factor.

Now as Capitalists we appreciate the dollar. We know that the best things in life are not free but are paid for by buying the time to be with family and friends. That a sunset is better when you have no monetary concerns. That great food tastes better when it is eaten in your awesome house instead of the crappy apartment. We all agree that money is a good thing, or else we wouldn't be in financial services. But excessive love of a dollar is dangerous.

Money is not the root of all evil. The unfettered adoration and pursuit thereof is.

Many of us in Financial Services are hyper competitive, and production is how we are measured and ranked. So it is expected that some could be corrupted to un-mitigated greed. Just don't let it be you, because that is the surest way to flame out overall. Better to make a little less but to make it for decade after decade and be sustainable. Think on this a bit.

So SAG is Stupidity times Arrogance times Greed.

$$S = S \times A \times G$$

If your Factor is above 2,000 you should really consider making some changes in yourself as you are at a high risk of failure, maybe even jailtime for ethical violations. You might want to reflect and calculate your SAG Factor quarterly and ask yourself how to bring it down to make sure you don't become avaricious and big headed and ultimately out of your career and money.

Now think about how this applies to clients. Doctors (specifically surgeons) are among the most arrogant people around, followed by engineers and lawyers (engineers because of intelligence and problem solving abilities, doctors because of their God Complex, attorneys because of a combination of both). Very high A scores. And Greed is universal.

You might want to do a quick SAG calculation when you meet a potential client, because it will be a good indicator of whether they will be a good client or a service nightmare.

We, The Sheeple

Or should we call this section "March of the Lemmings"?

Being Dutch, Dr. Stolk naturally has an affinity for windmills and tulips. We all know the story of how the first great modern bubble was the tulip, and at one point a single bulb was worth as much as a house on the canals of Amsterdam. Then **POP!**

In the 1990's the Dow Jones Industrial Average rose every single year. At one point it had three years in a row of 20%+ per year growth and five years of 16+% growth. And the New Economy was doing even better. So by 1999 everyone KNEW that 10+% per year stock market growth was normal, and that a conservative assumption of 6% per year compounded growth for planning was old fashioned.

POP! Worst market since The Great Crash, 50%+ loss on NASDAQ. Tech market meltdown.

Real Estate bubble.

POP!

Venture Capital.

POP!

What's next?

Bubbles are normal in the world of scarce resources. Because people are fueled by fear and greed. They are afraid of being poor, or that someone else is getting more than they are. The green-eyed monster of jealousy is powerful, and the madness of crowds a well-established phenomenon.

The Sheeple or Herd Mentality trap is insidious because most people in sales have had success by being agreeable folks, by not stirring the pot or be contrary during good times. It takes internal fortitude to ask "why is this" about the mores and assumptions that swirl around us.

It takes a very powerful True Self to be in orange when everyone else is wearing a dark blue suit, and to say "ummmm, not only does the emperor have no clothes, but we are heading for a train wreck because of the policies...."

Sometimes the crowd is right. 30 million Elvis fans can't be wrong as the old saying goes. But regularly asking yourself about the assumptions of the crowd, of why they think Justin Bieber is a musical genius, will prevent a huge mistake.

If you do what everybody else does all the time, you will get what everyone else gets.

If you always just go with the flow, you can be carried out to sea or over the edge of the cliff with the rest of the lemmings. Swimming against the crowd is difficult, but surviving a great crash is harder. Don't be seduced by "everybody knows".

Liked versus Respected

Do you think The Hoodie Bill Belichik cares if you like him or not?

News flash: he doesn't give a damn if anyone even on his own team likes him or not. But every single person in that organization RESPECTS him, as do his peers and competitors.

We all want to be liked. It makes things easier when people are friendly and smiling. And people **do** do business with people that they like and respect. But over the past few decades everyone has focused on the like part of the equation instead of the respect component.

Joe early in his career was lighting the world on fire, and part of it was because he didn't give a damn if you liked him but you were sure as hell going to respect him. He even told potential clients "I am going to tell you what you need to hear, not what you WANT to hear. You might not like it, but it is what a true professional should do." And by focusing on doing the right things he got respect, and was able to build decades long friendships with some of his clients. Worked so well he stopped doing it because management wanted to "polish" him.

Remember: swords have rough handles so you can get a grip.

Contrast this with the "professional visitors" who spend forever focusing on getting potential clients to LIKE them, so that they feel comfortable working with that advisor. Guess what, they can like you and never do business with you! How many "Likes" does a Facebook page or status have, and how many dollars does it translate to?

Action, not platitudes, are what gets the job done.

Yes, this attitude upsets some people (especially managers that are taught to make everyone happy instead of making people successful), but you will find that even though it can be slightly polarizing it is actually MORE effective than trying to please everyone. And production is what pleases management in the long run.

People buy into the New England/Belichik system. They know if they do their job they will have success. They have a chance to play for a Superbowl ring every year. Players don't care if Belichik is a grump because he is the best and demands that commitment from all around and so there is an attitude of winning, an edge of excellence surrounding Coach Belichik and all members of the organization.

Does your doctor really care if you like them? Are they going to spend hours talking with you and building the relationship so that you become comfortable with them and hopefully eventually listen to their advice? No way. They talk to you, assess the situation, and tell you "You need to lose 20 pounds, stop eating crap, buy some vegetables, get off your fat butt and join a gym or else you are going to have a heart attack and die. Here is a prescription, go fill it and see me in three months." And you do as she says. Well, maybe she has a bit better bedside manner than this, but that is still the underlying message and we follow doctor's orders. Maybe you should consider being more doctor and less friend…

Follow Them

Just so you know, Joe grew up on a beef farm so loves red meat. And because of the intense physical activity of distance running and Tae Kwon Do, he has a low iron count and was actually prescribed to eat more red meat. Yes, Virginia, there IS a Santa Claus!

So when Joe was a new Rep and still went out to meet clients at lunch instead of having it ordered in to his office so that he could control every aspect of the meeting dynamic (re-read that, as it could be very important) he met a potential client at the diner near the tech park that he was a regular at.

Being a Tuesday they had Buffalo Burgers. Like from bison. Very good meat, lean and tasty. Joe loves it and so of course he ordered a burger. Client was an artist at the video game company where everyone was Joe's client, brand new there, and got a salad.

They started talking, going through the financial planning process and things were going swimmingly. Then the food arrived. Joe took a big ol' bite of his burger, and the potential client turned green and almost puked.

Turns out he was not just a vegetarian but a very hard core vegan. Not for religious reasons, but still had an incredibly deep seeded belief system that Joe had just offended.

Obviously he never became a client of Joe's.

Lesson: let them go first always. If they order non-meat either follow their example or come right out and ask if it is ok for you to have meat, if it would offend them or not. If it wouldn't offend them they will tell you and if it would they will tell you too, and in either case you will have shown respect and it will be reciprocated. This will directly impact the Association score in the Trust Factor.

Same goes for ordering an alcoholic drink, unless you are specifically meeting for a cocktail.

So sometimes taking the lead is not the best thing.

Brain Games

You do the Sudoku puzzle every day, because it will help your brain. You sign up for Luminosity, to exercise your mind. You take nootropics so that your brain will function.

All bunk.

What?! A pair of hard core nerds that do over a thousand hours of research a year, that talk about Brain Business™ and harnessing and strengthening the mind, are poo-pooing these tools?

Yes. Because there is overwhelming evidence that shows that these tools are ineffective and expensive placebos.

Let's start with the puzzles. Unless you are struggling to do a puzzle, that it frustrates you and pisses you off and you feel like saying "forget it (or a stronger F word)!" then you aren't getting much benefit other than the basic enjoyment from the puzzle. If it is easy, it gives minimal benefit for brain development.

Let's take an example. Royal and Ambre. They are both mathematically inclined but Ambre is an engineer while Royal is in management so doesn't do nearly the amount of detail oriented pattern work of Ambre. Because of this, Ambre is drawn to doing Sudoku while Royal is drawn to more crosswords and games like Words with Friends that require creativity of limited resources and reacting to other's moves. While they would both get enjoyment from doing their particular activities, the benefits are limited because the games reinforce existing mental patterns instead of forcing growth (think Crossfit for brain by doing something different). Doing a Soduko could frustrate Royal and he might only be able to do a basic one as opposed to the most advance levels like Ambre, but the struggle is what makes it work. She should try a cross word puzzle.

Things like Luminosity have been shown to improve skill at clicking on a computer, or reaction time. And this is not to be ignored. But if you want to maintain the plasticity of your brain, to be more creative and have more mental focus, then do something hard and different. Try playing an instrument that you aren't used to. Use Dualingo or Pimsler or Rosetta Stone to learn a language, the harder the better. Listen intently to sitar music. Brush your teeth with your off hand. Take an art class, especially if you have the talent of a drunk toddler like Joe. Make it mentally tough, because your struggle is what earns you rewards in terms of brain functionality.

And a walk in the woods has been shown to be as good as anything else basically, because of the constantly changing perspectives and lack of parallel patterns. Think about the classic hallway in a college or office building: long straight lines, broken up by the perpendicular lines of the doorways. Same as a prison. Recent articles have pointed out how this pattern set (also reflected in many games on the computer) are unnatural and have a negative effect on the creativity and perception of the brain, instilling a malaise and laziness. This environment creates a prison for your mind.

Contrast this with the natural world, where trees are irregular in shape and size and pattern. Two steps and the mental input is completely different, needing to be reprocessed and assessed. Another two steps and another change. A ten-minute walk, even in familiar woods, will alter and enhance your thought patterns. Stretching the legs has benefits too.

Soooo about nootropics. Called "**smart drugs** or **cognitive enhancers**—are drugs, supplements, or other substances that improve cognitive function, particularly executive functions, memory, creativity, or motivation, in healthy individuals" to quote Wikipedia. It is over a $1B a year industry in the US.

News flash: placebo. Most of the time. Yes, the Nazis gave meth to their soldiers to improve their reaction time. Do you want to be a meth head Nazi?! Caffeine gives similar effects, improves cognitive function, and helps stave off Alzheimer's as well as repair some liver damage from alcohol consumption. Have a cup of Joe. Or five.

Lack of vitamins can have a negative effect on cognition and performance (especially Vitamin D, something frequently occurring in pale skinned Irish like one of the authors). But a balanced diet can help most people, supplemented with some basic multivitamins. Now we aren't medical doctors even though Dr. Stolk has military medical training. But for the vast majority of the people reading this book, a big cup of Joe and a cheap multivitamin a day plus a walk will be worth more than all the psuedo-science based fads.

Busy Vs Productive

This is a trap that many relatively new advisors fall into. "Oh man I am sooo busy! I spent five hours cold calling people and two hours doing research on something I'll never sell and one hour pushing paper. And I have three whole appointments this week!" Guess what kiddo? You are NOT paid to fill out paperwork. Nor are you paid by the number of dials you make to faceless names you know nothing about from some random list.

You are paid for results. Remember that. Paid. For. Results.

But results take time, and it can be very frustrating to keep four meetings in a day, get a dozen introductions, open a few cases and move along another one yet not make a dime that day. That is unless you embrace an activity driven model and measure the **right** activities, the fact finding and cases open and closing meetings and introductions that are at the core of the Granum System for building a successful Financial Services business.

Proper process leads to production.

If you want to really have hardcore analytics on your business read Granum's book "The Art and Science of Client Building" or the updated "Building a Financial Services Clientele". We would actually prefer if you read "Do You Want To Make MDRT, or Not?" for obvious reasons. Because we wrote that one. But what it comes down to is doing enough of the right activities on a daily basis that will allow you to build a successful business by applying the laws of large numbers to your activities. Let it be your guide.

Don't fall for the paper pushing trap. That is not the core of your business, it is totally ancillary. Paperwork should be done outside of the core business day (8-4) when you are either seeing people or fighting to see people.

Fill out the paperwork at nine at night, sitting on your couch with an adult beverage.

Run those analyses on the weekend in your comfy jammies listening to whatever you want so you can see people during the work day.

A dozen referred lead phone calls that take maybe 15 minutes to do are more effective than a half day of cold calls.

Do the right things to move your business, not just to fill time in the office.

Think of it this way: did you pass all those licensing exams to do $15 an hour work, like what people at McDonald's are going to get paid? Probably not, or else you have something seriously wrong upstairs. You want to make money, and serious cash. It's ok to admit that, it is the core of capitalistic societies and the impetus for advancement.

So if you had a chance to do $250 an hour work, why would you chose to do $15 an hour work? Especially mind numbingly boring stuff like filling out forms. You could be talking to people and making over ten times that rate and not want to impale yourself with your pen!

How about you focus on what the IRS calls "Highest and best usage", which is how they value land and other assets that are really more valuable than what they are being used for, like say a quarter acre lot with a small house in the middle of a city surrounded by thirty story buildings. BE the office building generating a million plus in net rents a month instead of the cute little house. Embrace the highest and best use of your time, and hire out the crap work.

Instead of cold calling for five hours and maybe getting two appointments (one or both of which will always blow you off), how about you invest 45 minutes into some research on a dozen potential clients, get someone in your network to introduce you to them, then spend fifteen minutes calling those dozen people? I guarantee you that on average the one hour of intelligent activity will yield more than the five hours of mindless dialing. This will free you up for four hours of doing your actual job: seeing people, and helping them secure their financial future by buying products from you.

The most effective Reps work the most intensely when they are working and don't screw around. First some numbers. Study by LIMRA (Life Insurance Marketing Research Association) a number of years ago found that those making MDRT (basically the benchmark for the industry representing roughly the top 10% of producers in the US, equaling about $100k of first year commissions in 2018) worked roughly 52 hours a week or so. And their utilization rate (percentage of the time that they were actually in front of a client instead of doing paperwork or dorking around like too many new advisors do) was around 50%. Meaning that these people that were averaging around $175k or so of revenue were actually doing their job about 26 hours a week.

Those Reps that were Court of the Table (3x the production level of MDRT, or ~$300k of first year commissions) were working a little more, about 55 hours or so a week. Pretty negligible really, only about a half an hour a day more. But their utilization rate was over 60%, meaning they were actually doing financial planning and selling for around 33 hours a week, or over an hour a day more than their peers that were MDRT. Keep in mind that Court of the Table producers were making gross probably around $500-$600k on average. They had staff that did the crap stuff you are doing, and more staff than the MDRT producers because an investment of $75k for an additional staff member would yield an additional $200k of revenue or so, for only an extra hour a day of the Rep's time. Good trade off.

Then we get to the Top of the Table producers, representing about 1/10th of 1% of those in financial services in the entire world. This is 6x the level of production of MDRT, or $600k+ of first year commissions. These people are usually at over a million of annual revenue and have more staff. But they actually work LESS than the Court of the Table producers or MDRT members in terms of hours per week: around 50. So a half hour a day less than the people making $100k first year commission. But the Top of the Table producers have utilization rates of around 70%, so when they are working they are either working with clients or managing their team that takes care of everything else. They are in front of clients on average just over 5 hours a day, the same amount of time that you are probably wasting each day.

Joe has produced at Top of the Table level. It is pretty awesome getting a six-figure paycheck one month. Much better than being broke and miserable because you are being busy doing nothing.

Wouldn't you rather work when you are supposed to work, and then be able to go have fun knowing that you actually busted your hump in the office, got done what needed to get done, and so have EARNED the right to party like a rock star?!

Just Once....

We've all had the thought "well, I don't really need to do x." Whether it is doing the notes immediately after a meeting or getting a full risk tolerance questionnaire or going through the investment statement line by line. Sometimes we just don't wanna. Could be we think the person won't become a client. Or we don't want to deal with the underwriting requirements. Or maybe it is because we don't want to wait weeks for the signature. Whatever it is.

Don't.

Don't take the shortcut.

Never give a client less than your best.

Forget legal/ethical issues and reasons like that which should be the ultimate guardrail.

Don't cheap your way out.

Because if you are doing someone's financial planning, that means no one else is.

Think about that.

If you don't do the job to the best of your ability and the needed standards, that family is going to fail, and it is 100% your fault because you were lazy.

"Just once" is that slippery slope. Never give in on your ethics, never do anything other than the right thing. Always. Because just once is once too many.

Pump Up the Volume!

The instant you hear the opening strains of Survivor's "Eye of the Tiger" from the Rocky movies (dun, dah duh dun, dah duh dun….) your heart starts to beat faster. You get excited, stimulated and ready to fight Ivan Drago AND Apollo Creed at once. Your entire demeanor changes, and you are ready to take on anyone or anything.

What would happen if you had the first thirty seconds of Eye of the Tiger on your phone and played it before going into a meeting? Maybe even assume the Champion Pose while doing so, channeling your inner Rocky. How would you walk into that meeting?

dun, dah duh dun, dah duh dun….

Can you feel the electricity as you get ready to compete, just from the MENTION of the opening beats?

Maybe you should give it a try this week, awakening your inner Champion with sound and action.

Blah Blah Blah

That is exactly what your client hears after about 30 seconds.

Because that is how our brains are wired.

Humans survived having no teeth or claws or armor by being able to determine quickly if something is a threat, lunch, or a potential mate quickly and then proceeding from that point by running, attacking, or fornicating. It was needed for the survival of the species, and we haven't really evolved much past that.

So if you get into minutiae, you are probably going to see the client's eyes glaze over because their mind has triaged you into the "boring" stack. Even an engineer can be put to sleep with details.

There are many ways to make sure that you stay engaged with the crocodilian part of the brain that is the initial processing center for the mind. In fact, our forthcoming book Brain Business ™ contains multiple chapters and goes extremely in depth on the subject. So for now be content with this concept: be unexpected. Be different. Make their brain work to figure you out, through questions or unusual things that make them stop and actually think instead of moving on autopilot. Orrin Klaff gives a great overview in "Pitch Anything". Check it out.

This vignette is short and to the point, blunt even because we want you to now take a minute and write in the space below ideas for throwing a curve to the client, of shocking them to engage them. Go ahead, take all of three minutes. You will thank us later.

APPENDIX A: Models

If you are of a certain age, the instant we sing "I'm a model and you know what I mean..." you picture some bald British guys. But we mean a different sort of model, no matter how cool "Right Said Fred" was for a few months. NOT going to do a turn on the catwalk...

If you didn't know, Joe was a physicist by training. Total geek. And as a physicist he always looked for models to help explain the complexity of the world in simple terms. And as Albert Einstein said, if you can't explain something to a six-year-old you don't understand it well enough. So hopefully we explain some of these concepts in a way that you can then relay to your clients as they can definitely help you in your business.

And you should review the True Self/False Self Model from **It's a Trap!** as it is a model that you will be able to utilize beyond your financial services career.

Not Paying Taxes...

This concept Joe used with every single client and is one of the centerpieces of his financial planning philosophy. Here is the concept verbatim (you might want to memorize it, if and only if you want clients to work with you):

> "Not paying taxes is better than paying taxes."

There are legal and ethical ways to minimize your tax bill. As the financial advisor you have a responsibility to your client to assist them with tax favored strategies so that they keep more of what they make, whether from income of investments. Yes, it is a very Libertarian sounding concept but ask anyone with a brain (no matter their political affiliation) if they could save a million dollars in taxes just by doing what they would have anyway but filling out one page of documents to get the legal tax shielding, they would all say yes. Because they are human. It is how we are programed, if we weren't this way we wouldn't have survived.

Now when you draw the above symbol and explain the meaning, that not paying taxes is better than paying taxes, you need to back it up. Whether it is utilizing 408 plans or section 7702 plans or a NIMCRUT, you really should have a handful (or more) of ideas to make sure that you create tax efficiency or savings for your client. Which leads us into...

Seeds Versus Harvest

If you have to pay tax on the weight, do you want to not pay taxes on the seed but then pay tax on the entire weight of your harvest? Or would you rather pay on the weight of the seed packet instead of the watermelons? Because this is one of the most common financial mistakes advisors recommend to clients. Suzie Orman and Dave Ramsey regularly tell callers to do this. On a side note, we wonder if those two yahoos are going to be subject to the DOL Fiduciary Rule, because they certainly are giving advice. Bad advice, but still advice.

Every time a professional (usually the CPA due to their short sightedness) tells a client to max out their 401k, they are creating a future tax issue. For a really in depth analysis on this read Ed Slott's book "The Retirement Savings Time Bomb". And yes, Ed is a CPA, one of the few that sees the big picture instead of just this year's tax return.

Why is maxing the 401k a bad idea? Two words: tax leverage.

Doesn't matter who you voted for in the last Presidential Election, tax rates are going to have to go up. Our national debt hit TWENTY TRILLION DOLLARS in 2017. That is:

$20,000,000,000,000

That is five times our annual federal budget.

Social Security is going broke.

We are fighting SEVEN undeclared wars as this is written. Could be eight by the time you read it.

The only way we could afford the Bush era tax cuts (and additional Medicare spending) was if we continued to have strong economic growth. Needless to say, didn't happen. But we still have a decent chunk of the lowered tax rates from the past thirty years of tax cuts.

Our debt essentially doubled to over $61,000 per person under Obama.

The Congressional Budget Office (which is non-partisan) says that we need to raise tax rates by roughly 50% just to cover our current and known obligations. Think about that.

Fifty percent.

So if you are paying 30% right now, you'll be going to 45% or so. Which rate do you want to pay, since you have to pay taxes at some point?

Oh, and as you get more experienced (or your clients do) and accumulate wealth, you probably climb tax brackets. Your clients being in a 50%+ income tax bracket in retirement is a high probability.

So yeah, max out that 401k now to avoid the 40% current taxation just to have them pay 60%+ down the road. I'm sure they have no issue with taking money from their older selves that they were planning on using with their grandchildren and sending it down to Washington DC. Go ahead and ask them.

And in case you doubt our assertions, here is some math to back it up. You can do this calculation with your client so they understand the future issues and will work with you to avoid them if you can communicate the concept of seeds versus harvest.

Assumptions:

30% Current Tax rate

45% Future Tax rate

9% growth rate

30 years of growth

$7k pre-tax contribution

$4900 post tax contribution

401k gross balance: $1,000,055

401k net: $555,030

Roth balance: $700,039

Additional taxes paid because of bad advice: $145,009

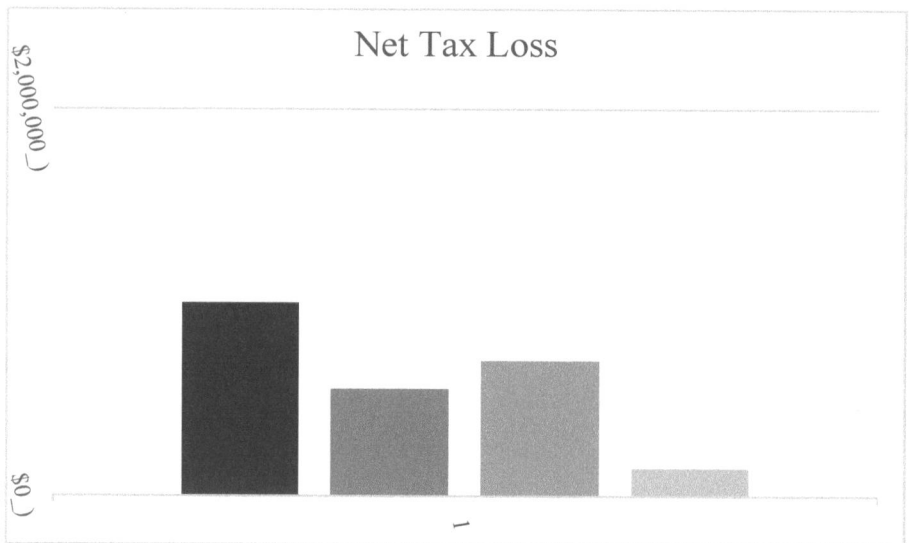

Calculations performed via the bankrate.com calculators, so you can take your client to the site and have them input the numbers and see the difference for themselves so they truly believe.

Wedding Cake Theory of Insurance

Life insurance requirements are dynamic, evolving over the life of the client. As a new college grad, the only needs at that point generally are to cover debt (such as the average of $60k+ of combined student loans and consumer debt that is out there now). Not that big of a deal really. But when the client has a spouse and 2.5 kids and a minivan and mortgage, the need is much higher for a time. The life insurance coverage should reflect this.

One of the things you should do as the planner is keep in mind the words of Wayne Gretzky, the greatest hockey player to ever lace up skates (with apologies to Pittsburgh Penguins fans, as Super Mario just didn't do it for essentially two decades of dominance): "a good hockey player plays where the puck is. A great hockey player plays where the puck is going to be." Gretzky had tremendous ice vision and seemingly was two strides ahead of everyone else because of this. Be a great one for your clients with their planning and help them understand and lay the groundwork for where they will be.

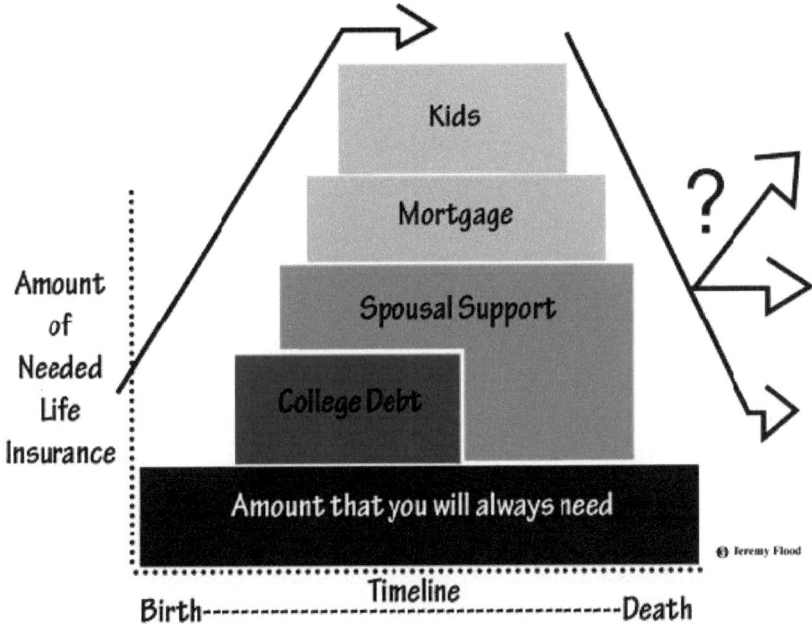

There is a base level of coverage that everyone should have, even children. Joe has insurance on his boys, not necessarily to cover the costs if anything happens to them, but because he would be a completely useless wreck and unable to generate income for at least half a year. So there is coverage on the kids to cover costs, but more so to give Joe time to heal. These policies the boys will take over when they get out of college, and will help them with their future. The cash value will be a good asset for them to start their careers, and all of the policies have the guaranteed right to purchase more insurance no medical questions asked. This is a big deal in case the kids develop any issues: Joe has laid the groundwork for his grandchildren to be taken care of wayyy out in the future.

The first big layer on the cake is when your client gets debt. Car, college, home: all of these produce a big step up in need. So as someone moves along from left to right through time, you probably have jumps in need around 18, 21, and 30 years old or so. These jumps are by the amount of the debt plus 10% to cover miscellaneous costs. Yes, these needs will change, but we are trying to cover the concepts.

Then when your client gets married, you have a jump of the amount needed by the value of their spouse's take home pay. So use the $1M=$2k/mth calculation. Add 10% just to be safe, more if you need extra security to sleep at night. Some people might say "Well, they can remarry." Or "We don't need all that." They probably do need it, because people either spend all the money that their spouse earns, or they are saving it for a purpose. So that income probably needs to be replaced. And, there is always the time needed to heal. Having the ability to take the time they need, without financial worry, is definitely of great value, so imbed a little of it into your planning for them. **Having extra money rarely hurts.** (As to the remarry thing: do you want to force them to have to remarry for money, or would you rather have them do it for love? Unless you are a cold hearted bastard, sell the insurance so they can make the choice. If they aren't willing to do so, just tell them to go file for the divorce now, it'll cost less to do so now.)

Then they have kids. Use the same sort of calculation to cover day care and other expenses, plus costs of college and other things (Sweet 16, braces, a trip to Disneyland when they turn 10, whatever is important to you). That is the maximum amount of insurance they will probably need. The top of the cake.

As debt is paid off, the need for life insurance steps down. As kids get through college, those needs step down too. No longer need the insurance that was covering this, so you can get rid of it. The need never goes down to zero, but is not at the same level as when you have a new spouse, house, and baby.

Sort of looks like a wedding cake, doesn't it?

Now, any of these needs that are "short term" i.e. ten years or less should only be covered with term insurance. Any needs of 20 years or greater are most effectively covered by permanent insurance. Anything in between depends on the need and other parts of the financial picture such as cash flow, retirement savings, financial aid considerations, etc and is where you as the advisor truly add value.

If you know they are going to have some long-term needs develop in the future, you may want to start covering them now with some permanent coverage. It will cost less if you don't wait, and the insurance policies will have some time to accumulate value. It also builds future flexibility into the planning, something that in the dynamic workforce environment we have cannot be understated.

Note that way out to the right has question marks for this very reason. We have trouble telling the weather a week out, how can we with too much certainty know what a client's future looks like 40+ years down the road? It is hubris to belief otherwise. All we can do is give them flexibility in case of:

1. Estate taxes. Will probably always be around, and if your client is successful you can address part of this tax bill before it even develops.
2. Pension maximization. OK, not a ton of people have pensions but those that do buy a ton of life insurance as it is more cost effective and flexible than taking joint and survivor options at work.
3. Private pension. OK, really annuity. But a cash values life insurance plan can always be converted into an income stream with minimal tax concerns.

4. Additional savings bucket. Maybe your client doesn't want to touch another asset yet, the cash value in the life insurance can give them an option to wait. Or maybe they need the asset because they didn't listen to you and don't have enough saved.

5. Retirement replacement tool. Typically one spouse will pre-decease the other by a number of years. Having life insurance to replace all the money the client and spouse spent having fun with each other while they were around maximizes the utility and memories, which ultimately is what money is. At the first death, the life insurance re-fills the coffers so the survivor can enjoy the rest of their golden years and have less "what if?'s".

6. Legacy planning. Could be a great gift for the grand kids.

7. Charity.

So sit down with the client and draw out this Wedding Cake and ask them point blank: where are you on here right now? Do you believe that you have done the right planning, with the right products, for where you are now and in the future?

Trust Factor:

The initial iteration of this model is taken from "The Trusted Advisor" by Maister, Green, and Galford. This was one of the most influential books on Joe's career, and something he has noodled on for over a decade. More like obsessed over, and John has picked up a bit of it too.

Joe has lectured all over the country on the subject and teaches an ethics continuing education course on "The Art and Science of Trust" where he does in depth case studies on the individual components and helps professionals develop approaches to improve on each metric with the outcome being a much more effective business. You might want to attend this session at some point, but only if you want tremendous growth in production from a firm ethical foundation. Or need Ethics CE to keep your licenses, that too.

But based on over a decade of additional experience and research, the initial model put forward by Maister, Green, and Galford needs to be improved upon a little, adding an additional factor. So instead of discussing the initial equation we present here and now for the first time the Enhanced Trust formula.

$$T= (C + R+ I +A)/SO$$

C = Credibility

R = Reliability

I = Intimacy

A = Association

SO = Self Orientation

First and foremost note that the output is inversely proportional to the Self Orientation of the professional. This embodies Joe's concept of Economic Altruism that is codified by the Rotarian motto of "Givers Get." Working on yourself, becoming less self-centered and more client caring, is the single most effective way to radically alter the trust level with the people you interact with. Chew on that for a moment.

C is Credibility. Do you know what you are talking about? Are you a CFP®? Do you exude confidence because you have practiced your language and have 30 years of martial arts? Are you a NAIFA and MDRT member? Did you write the book? Then WHY should they listen to you?!

R is Reliability. Do you do what you say, when you say it? How awesome is your staff? Are you late for the meeting? Do you always provide a consistent level of experience? Which version of you are they getting today?

Intimacy is **I**. How well do you know your client? How well do they know you? Have they shared experiences and insights with you that they haven't with anyone else? Do you know their WHY and they know yours? Maybe you should review some of the fact-finding questions from earlier in this book, because they will help you become more intimate with the client than any other professional in their world.

A is for Association. Where you there in the tough times when they were getting started, or did you just show up to pick the fruit of other's labor? When they think about your past together, did you dine and ditch or do your share and more? When they think about why they are successful, are you associated with that memory or do they associate you with more negative things, losses and mistakes? Do they associate you with the right actions or cutting corners? Guilt by Association, or world class?

Keep in mind there are different contexts for trust: you can trust Dr. Stolk on a military operation but not to teach a painting class. Joe can remember every aspect of sections of the tax code and the usage thereof, but like many a physicist is awkward in social situations and should never be allowed in a golf club. So you might trust someone as a surgeon or attorney but not let them watch your kids. And vice versa. Trust is situational.

Each factor gets a 1-10 assignment, and remember the CLIENT's perception is what matters, whether true or not. For the components on the top of the equation 1 is lowest end (like you couldn't even pass your basic licensing exams and just got out of prison on Credibility and are a total dumpster fire on Reliability, basically like Dory from "Finding Nemo"). 10 is the highest: you have four sets of letters after your name, you wrote multiple books on the subject, you are a sought after talking head on TV and radio, and are recognized as one of the world's leading experts. As John would say: the only way that Joe could be a 10 is with his brain and experience because he has a face made for radio!

Again note that the bottom of the equation, the Self Orientation, is inversely proportional to your Trust Factor. This means that a single point swing on this will have tremendous effect on the outcome of dealing with the client. A 1 is the best you can have here: you are literally like the Buddha or a holy person that gives of themselves to others without thought. The military is built off of low Self Orientation of the men and women serving because they believe the mission is more important than themselves; they can and do make the ultimate sacrifice for the good of others. A 10 on SO means that you are a total conman or woman only out for yourself and you would sell your own mother without blinking an eye if it benefitted you. Horrible human being! You should be sitting in a jail cell next to certain people we know....

Each client also has a particular value of the Trust Factor at which point they will do business with you. This is something inherent in them. Some people are more trusting than others, some have become jaded after being burned. And other sales people are among the most trusting and easy to sell.

So take a half an hour with a piece of paper and calculate your Trust Factor. Then list one thing you can do to improve each of the components. This exercise could be the single most valuable thing in this book. Imagine the improvement in all aspects of your business if your clients all trusted you more.

Three Phase Retirement Model

OK, time to talk about the R word. This is one of the most stressful emotional times for an American because so many define who they are by what they do. Take away the job title and the mission and they are lost, foundering, and without a purpose. This can have serious negative health effects. Part of your job as a planner is to help mitigate these and other risks.

On a side note, we are amazed by the number of people who start thinking about retirement way too late, like under a year before they want to retire. Business owners are among the worst, because their entire lives are built around the business, it is usually their single greatest asset, and they typically have spent years maximizing personal cash flow and deductions instead of business valuation and processes to make it transitionable. So they suddenly flip the switch and say "OK, I want to retire soon", but need two or even five years to get the business ready to sell. It is like coming home one day and deciding you want to move and putting a "For Sale By Owner" sign out the next morning. A few weeks of planning and strategic improvements will dramatically increase the value of the home. A business much more so.

With two to three years of guidance Dt. Stolk often doubles or even triples the value of the business. Joe wishes he could get returns like that! But the effect of it is the client has more money for the planning ideas Joe develops, and the pie is so much larger that the delayed gratification is worth it for client and advisors. If you have business owners in your book of business, you might want to consider calling Dr. Stolk because leveraging his professional skills will make your client much better off and make you the hero. With a bigger check.

So back to retirement.

This is what retirement looks like now for many people.

3 PHASES OF RETIREMENT

As opposed to the old model of hitting 65, getting the gold watch and pension from the company you have been with for forty years, and you start having fun and playing with grandkids and slowly inflation and age eat away at your lifestyle over the next 12 years then you drop dead while playing bingo in Florida. So why has our model of retirement changed?

First off, almost no one works for the same company for more than a decade unless that company is a governmental agency or entity like the Military, a school district, or some other tax payer supported organization. Those people also get a pension usually which will cover the majority of their retirement planning and remove longevity risk. Nice deal.

Longevity risk cannot be overlooked. 200 years ago life expectancy for a man was 47. One hundred years ago it was upper 50's. Baby Boomers that are hitting retirement age now have a life expectancy of 25 more years for a male, almost 30 for a female. Gen X'ers could have almost 40 years as medical science keeps extending lifespans. Think about that: retirements lasting as long as the working career. Huge difference from the days when you worked until you died or got eaten by the sabertooth tiger.

Secondly, we no longer have the three-legged stool of pension, Social Security, and personal wealth to create income in retirement. Social Security benefits have lagged behind inflation for decent income earners, and the annual increases in benefits post retirement have continuously fallen behind inflation for decades and will continue to do so. This has shifted more and more of the onus to the individual, a trend that even with recent legislation in California does not look like it will change much.

Third, grandma and grandpa no longer live in the next town. Chances are your clients will end up being relatively far from their family. So the traditional caregiver role is changed, as well as the cost of travel throughout retirement. There is also the issue of changing states for tax or long term care planning purposes.

Fourth is the emergence of long term care needs. That heart attack that killed your grandfather at 74?? Now they fix 'em up and he is back on the golf course two weeks later. And has another heart attack at 82, when he falls and breaks his hip. They fix that too but he can't live on his own so needs a facility for the next three years. At $7,500 a month.

Or mom develops Alzheimer's disease, and can't be on her own. But she lives four states away. So she goes into a semi-residential home at $4,000 a month, then transitions to the more skilled facility after five years (and a quarter million dollars) that is $100,000 a year for the next three and a half years.

Over half of those aged 65 today will need long term care at some point.

Meaning you had better plan on it for your clients. Because nothing will destroy an investment portfolio faster than $100k+ a year of draw-downs that were not expected, sucking away cash and dignity. Probably a good time to go review Long Term Care Insurance, as it is one of the best hedges you as an advisor can make against having

116

to pull assets from the market at a not great time. Plus it protects YOUR income stream.

So back to our current model of retirement.

We are going to introduce a concept called PRL. This is Pre-Retirement Lifestyle, and refers to the amount of after tax money that is spent doing what the client does. This ranges from cost of shelter (could be home ownership, renting an apartment, living exclusively on a cruise ship year round, whatever), food, medical costs, spoiling grandkids, etc. Whatever their lifestyle is in the few years before retirement. PRL is different for different people and that is totally ok.

Once you determine an after tax annual dollar amount for PRL in whatever your base year is (today, or year of retirement if different), this number then is adjusted for inflation so that we are always talking about "buying power", which is the important thing. Your client won't care if everything is 10x as expensive twenty years from now if your planning still allows them to live their life at that point without financial worry.

Now when your clients retire, guess what? It's party time! They have money, don't have to go to work the next day, have their health, and it's all new. That trip to Disney they always wanted? Book it Danno! Same with getting the golf club membership and taking the cruise and seeing what they want and trying new restaurants and all that. It is a vacation that they have been waiting for for thirty years. The grandchildren love this stage.

Many professionals will continue to work part time, doing consulting. This can create income to offset the rapid spend rate and should be included in your calculations if appropriate. Or don't count on the revenue and use it as play money. Others do a ton of volunteering, giving back to causes they believe in. Not for profits love this stage because these are among their most active volunteers, providing a significant amount of hours that the organizations could not afford to pay for.

If you have not taken a look at Tom Hegna's book "Paychecks and Playchecks" (or at least looked at the www.tomhegna.com website) for some of his research and insight, you are missing a lot of valuable information that could help you help your clients. Might want to do so.

The PRL that we determined earlier for your client? Use 1.5x that here, unless they had a very high lifestyle to begin with and then you can be a little more conservative. But every day is vacation, is that dream of the golden years with spouse and family and enjoyment. This is literally what they worked and saved for for decades, so plan for them to enjoy it without regret. These dollars will bring the most joy of any that are spent in retirement in aggregate (concept of highest marginal utility from economics) and as such you as the planner should be able to look them in the eye and say "Go for it!". This is the time when memories are made, so we are at Peak Lifestyle.

The Go-Go Stage typically lasts somewhere between 8 and 12 years, depending on the person. It might also take a hiatus, especially if one spouse gets sick as happened with Joe's parents. A year long cancer battle forces a short term period of Slow Go, but often afterwards the client will pop back up into the Go-Go once the person is in remission or passes on. Joe's dad had periods of both of these, and is once again in Go-Go (albeit close to the tail end).

But the excitement gets old after a while. After playing the same hole at the golf club four days a week for the first two years, it loses its mystery and the client drops to attending the club twice a week. After the third trip to Disney, the kingdom isn't so magic. And as the grandchildren become teenagers they aren't as much fun.

There is also the physical effects. That robust 66 year old at 72 has lost a half step very often, and by 77 it is a full step. If not your client, then some of their family and friends have had health issues, maybe even passed on and slowly (or suddenly) your client is not concerned as much with their enjoyment because they start seeing the fragility of live. They start getting worn down a bit by the emotional and physical burden of caring for others maybe. Instead of a cruise meeting new people, they'd rather have a dinner party with the friends they've had for decades.

The combination of all of these things means your client transitions into the second stage of retirement, the Slow-Go Phase. They are still active, just not as much. Instead of getting a new car every three or four years, they say "ah, I'm not driving that much" and keep it for an extra year or two. They blow off a charity golf tournament because it is going to rain. They stop one of their volunteer activities because they are a little tired. They stop consulting because they feel they are losing their edge, or their contacts are all retiring. They start saying good bye to more friends and family as their circle starts to shrink as people their own age pass on.

In terms of cash-flow we have returned to pretty close to PRL, the Pre-Retirement Lifestyle. The first parts of this phase are a quieter version of the years leading up to retirement, but with more reflection. Religion tends to become more important, as does mending fences. Especially with family.

The time in Slow-Go is determined more by physical/mental capacity than the others. If a client is physically robust and mentally acute they rarely decide "ya know, I'm X years old. Time to just sit on my front porch and be a grumpy old man." Because that giving up of activity is the surest way to a shorter lifespan. If you are calculating for client, this period will last from the end of your determined Go-Go Phase to life expectancy, and maybe 2-3 years beyond. It is

119

heavily dependent on their activity levels as that is one of the greatest determinants of robustness in this stage.

Funny how activity will determine YOUR success early in your career and your long-range potential, and will do the same with your clients in retirement. The larger your network in each case, the better and longer. You might want to chew on that thought for a moment or three.

In terms of financial numbers, the inflation adjusted after-tax cash-flow is generally close to that of a few years before retirement if the client has a traditional job and wasn't trying to stack hours for a pension calculation.

The final stage of retirement is the No-Go or Maintenance Stage. Given the advances in medical science we literally have no clue how long this period will last. Joe had two great aunts live past 99. Or it could even never happen, especially if your client decides in the Go-Go stage to race cars like John intends to do and go out in a blaze of glory. But running out of money is a fear you can alleviate.

This stage literally is a slow decline to the inevitable end.

If Alzheimer's is involved (like with Joe's grandparent's) it could be a decade of more of watching the person disappear while their body is still here.

A majority of a person's medical expenses for their entire life are spent in this stage.

Other than medical expenses and housing, there is not much cost in this stage. Food, but there is typically not a huge expense as appetite wanes over time for all things. Shouldn't be driving so car costs are non-existent. The income level here level is only 75% of the PRL or so and ramps down to 50% or so, but with a pair of caveats.

The first is that long term care is critical at this stage. The client almost definitely needs it, and the lack of coverage is one of the quickest ways to suck away a lifetime of savings and destroy the legacy they wanted to create for future generations. It is also one of the quickest ways to harm the future generations as kids sacrifice their careers and economic future to take care of Mom (the majority of the time women outlive men). Contributions to retirement are scaled back and college savings stop as the kids take care of the parent(s). Long Term Care Insurance will completely eliminate this risk. And as the advisor you have an obligation to address it. It will also keep them as a client because they will still have a portfolio to invest.

The second caveat is longevity risk. This No Go period could last three months. It could last three decades. We literally have NO CLUE with any person, and medical advancements are making the average tenure here longer and longer. Insurance tables used to endow at 90, then 100. Now 120. Every decade they have to extend them, because people are living longer. The only way to completely remove this risk of outliving the money (if no pension) is an annuity producing a baseline of guaranteed income. It's a non-debatable mathematical fact.

So let's review what our 3 Phase Retirement Model looks like again,

3 PHASES OF RETIREMENT

with the PRL numbers on it so that it is embedded in you for future discussion with clients.

BULLSEYE!

The average human being can remember somewhere between 400-500 names and faces at any one time. This is part of the reason many school districts try to keep the grade schools below this level, as it aides in the social development of the children.

Within this outer circle of contact is a smaller circle of around 150 of the people that you interact with regularly. This is a combination of work, social, neighborhood, family, etc. You actually know something about these people, more than just a quick wave across the parking lot. They will lend you their hedge trimmers or have a beer with you, or sit and talk during the kids' soccer game.

Then we have the Christmas Card list group. You know their spouse and kids names, if you ran into each other at the airport you would talk and probably grab a bite together. Typically you have some shared experiences beyond working for the same place or kids in school together. You probably have had more than a few cups of coffee (or something stronger) together. This is generally about 50 or 60 people.

50-60

This is where you want to get introductions to generally as the level of relationship, either now or in the past, is sufficiently strong enough that your client's opinion matters. Generally for the larger outer circle, the relationships are too tenuous to be of much use (but are still better than a cold call. Anything is better than a cold call!).

Inside of the Christmas Card Circle is the Dinner Group. These are the 20 or 30 people in a client's world that they would chose to have dinner with or go grab a coffee/drinks with on a semi-regular basis. These people tend to have longer and or deeper/more intense relationships with your client then the Christmas Card group and are current so relevant. If not family, they are often professional associates that are also friends, and there is more of a respect factor coming into play in this subset that is not as apparent in the outer circles. This is the most valuable circle in terms of combination of size and ease of developing as clients. Think about it: if you got five introductions per meeting with your client into this space, you would probably never run out as membership in this circle evolves with your client's position in life. As they climb the ladder, who they invest their time with does so too. Focus your efforts in this space and you will be rewarded.

Then we have the Bullseye in the middle of the target. These are the handful of people that are in the innermost circle of the client. This is where you can call Dr. Stolk and say "Templin wants us to talk" and it doesn't matter what it is about, you have the meeting because of that relationship (do not call John up and abuse this! Remember, he **does** know how to find you and do bad things to you). This is where if you called any of our handful of people in this space they would talk with you because of the power of that relationship.

You probably will not get to Innercircle introductions with your clients for a while because it takes time to earn these, but this is the ultimate goal. And you will be surprised as to who is in this place for certain clients: you can potentially meet some powerful men and women through one of their closest friends that you will never discover by reading Forbes or the Financial Times. But after enough work and personal connection with you they reveal that they are close buddies with XYZ rock star or business leader or politician or their godmother sits on the Board of Q. These wll reveal themselves to you over time as you prove worthy.

Tithing and Elephant Hunting

If you are religious you have definitely heard of tithing, where you give 10% of your annual income to your church to support it. You probably have even heard the concept in general. Let's extend it from your income though to something that eventually you will realize is even more valuable: time.

126

10% of your time is a big deal. On a professional weekly basis that is 5+ hours (yes, we are assuming you are working at least 50 hours a week). You should be dedicating roughly 5-10% of your time to booking new business (dialing for dollars as we used to call it. But again, please don't cold call as it is literally less efficient than standing on a street corner dressed like Uncle Sam wearing a sandwich board that says "Financial Freedom: Talk 2 ME!"). This is the part of your day that feeds all the other activities so is the most valuable. DO NOT SHIRK THIS!!!

You should be giving 10% equivalent time to charity work (NOT during the business day until you have built a business that runs independent of you). This will have a positive influence on your Self Orientation score for the Trust Factor. This volunteer work will make you not only a better human being but a better producer. Think about that.

10% of your day should be spent running your business. This is where you think and act like the CEO instead of the on staff financial planner. This is where you meet with staff to make sure your systems are running right and deals are flowing through your processes, that there are no bottle necks (which are typically you as the Advisor). That the work is getting done, but also thinking about the process of the work to maximize its dollar value to your shareholders (you, partners, family, etc). Working ON the business, not IN the business as Michael Gerber would say.

Big thing: you should also only dedicate the equivalent of 10% of your professional time to elephant hunting. What is elephant hunting you may ask? That is going after big game. The cases that change your economic outlook. Too many Reps chase the big payday exclusively instead of spending enough time on "basic cases" that build your skills, revenue, and business. They go for the sexy instead of the profitable.

Joe has written more than a handful of life insurance cases that had over six figures of commissionable base premium. These are all elephants. There is a lot of meat on an elephant, but they aren't easy to hunt, especially if you only have a bow and arrow and spears as you might have right now due to your knowledge base and experience.

The gestation period of an elephant is about two years.

None of these cases are quick to develop, and if you spend all your time chasing elephants early in your business you will be out of business because you will starve in the interim.

So dedicate 10% of your time hunting elephants, but the bulk (over half) building a sustainable core business that you can predict revenues from. Think of it as farming: if you plant today you know in 6-8 weeks you will have food enough to sustain you. So plant every day so that you can survive and grow even (remember, excess grain becomes beer!) yet also tithe your time towards hunting the big game because a big case once a quarter will generate your profit and growth.

$1M = $2k

So remember when we stated that $1mm of asset could be converted to $2k a month of cash-flow, after tax, adjusted for inflation? Let's take a moment to lay that out so that you can have it in your head and show a client on the back of a napkin and look impressive.

First, remember that you have an obligation to the client to err on the side of conservative. Which is meaning that they have more money. Because they will not be too upset if they have a little extra, but if grandma goes broke you bet that the wolves (and attorneys) will be knocking on your door.

First, we have to agree that we want income generated. If we were going pure long range growth we could go all equities because short term volatility is not so important when the asset is not to be touched for 20+ years.

Second, we need to agree that yes, part of this portfolio is not going to be touched for 20+ years, so we need growth to offset the effect of inflation.

Third, we need to agree that time IS our ally, because it allows us to do things like tax shield parts of the portfolio to further leverage opportunities. We will keep some cash in the portfolio to always have some flexibility and will give up a sliver of growth potential for peace of mind.

And fourth, we need to agree that even once we have the fundamental framework in place, we will tweak regularly because that is what is needed to make sure the client's family is ok.

So let's agree that your investment mix will be somewhere along the lines of:

4% Cash

3% Real Estate

10% Bonds

35% Large Companies

25% International Companies

15% Midsize Companies

8% Small Companies

Go ahead and argue "well, my model says 3.5% cash and 33% Large Company, and I break out junk bonds from corporates and..."

Whatever. We are trying to get a rough idea for a rule of thumb, not trying to design a nuclear reactor.

Cash has historically done a bit over 4.5%.

Bonds 7.5% for 10 Year Treasuries. Corporates have done about 150 to 200 basis points above this.

For both Bonds and Cash let's knock 2% off for our safety factor (like a good engineer), which puts us in line with the current historical lows. So 2.5% for Cash return and since our Bonds are a mix of Government, Corporate (Investment and some Junk) and International, 6.5% is reasonable and conservative.

Since 1950 the S&P 500 has done just about 11%. This is from Standard & Poors so should be a good reflection, but to be safe knock a point off and assume 10% for US Large Caps.

Real Estate (like REITS, not your own house) has historically performed closer to an equity than a bond, so using only 8.0% is reasonable too.

International has outperformed US by over a percent per year. So 11% with our safety factor built in.

Mid-Sized outperform Large Cap by same amount. Small Caps outperform by an additional 1.5%, but let's give it only 1% as we are really conservative.

So putting it all in a nice table:

ASSET	Return	Weight	Weighted Return
Cash	2.5%	0.04	0.10%
Bonds	6.5%	0.10	0.65%
Real Estate	8.0%	0.03	0.24%
Large US	10.0%	0.35	3.50%
International	11.0%	0.25	2.75%
Mid-Sized	11.0%	0.15	1.65%
Small Cap	12.0%	0.08	0.96%
Blended		1.00	9.85%
Net of 35% Tax			6.40%
Net of 4% Inflation			2.40%

And that boys and girls is why a million dollars is only worth $2,000 of income a month.

Deflector Shield

It's a Trap! That battle station is fully operational!

OK, we had to get another Star Wars line in the book someplace because the publisher required us to.

But if you have watched Rogue One (or any of them) recently, you know that a deflector shield is an energy based defensive projection that surrounds an object (typically a ship) to protect it. Even the second Death Star had a deflector shield to protect it from the Rebellion scum…

Think about the energy requirements of a fully operational battle station. You have life support, which is critical and takes up like five percent of the total power. You have offensive weapons, which can take up ten plus percent of the energy needs. More for certain ships. Propulsion is the majority of the need as ships from small X Wing fighters up to the Star Killer base need to move quickly over immense distances.

You probably think we are touched in the head even having this discussion, but here is the thing: almost everyone has seen Star Wars and will know what you are talking about. More people understand the basics of the Force than finance. So if they already have a basis of knowledge to draw from, use it.

But one of the most critical parts of all of these ships is the deflector shield. Without it, a turbolaser would rip them apart like a Rancor with an R2 unit. OK, that was overly geeky. A single blast would depressurize the ship and kill everyone, rendering the most powerful weapons vulnerable to being destroyed by the smallest hits.

Do you have a deflector shield for your clients to protect them? Do they allocate 5% of the energy of their ship for protection? What would 5% of your client's annual income dedicated to life insurance so for them? Doesn't how powerful an offensive weapon (investments) it is, if the small unprotected exhaust port triggers a chain reaction and wipes everything out. A deflector shield, 5% of the energy, would have protected everything else.

OK, we got the nerdiness out of our system. Actually, now we are going to go to the extreme of nerdy. Hold on to your pocket protectors and double tape your glasses!

Mueller-Templin Simplification Ratio

Life Insurance as a financial planning tool has been around longer than the United States, dating to the early Roman times, evolving through the era of the Dutch East India Company (as Stolk likes to point out whenever possible), and truly coming into its own in England at the height of its Empire. The idea of utilizing the laws of large numbers and probability to predict mortality and mitigate the individual risks thereof has created industries and fortunes while simultaneously protecting families and small businesses the world over. As a whole, the life insurance industry represents almost $850 billion of revenue in the US alone, with over $20.1T of benefits in force (2015 Life Insurer Fact book by LIMRA).

The earliest income tax code in the US was introduced in 1913 to generate revenue based upon economic lessons learned during the Spanish American War. It was 13 pages long. Shorter than this section of the book. Even this nascent kernel to the current 74,608 page byzantine tome (as of 4/15/16) had a special and explicit endorsement of life insurance as a valuable contribution to the social good, deserving of protection from the Washington leaching of taxation.

The internal cash surrender value of a whole life policy is designed as a terminal reserve to allow levelization of premiums over the scheduled payments of the policy: essentially overpayments in the early years creates excesses to ensure that future premiums at advanced ages do not increase or even need to be paid in the case of limited payment policies. This acceleration of cash flows creates a reserve account that equals the death benefit at endowment of the policy under the traditional design parameters, and in earlier years is a cash equivalent asset to the policy owner. This asset is excluded from income tax under Section 101a or 101j of the Internal Revenue Code as long as it meets the definitions in Section 7702 of Life Insurance.

Combine the tax-free nature of the insurance asset with the predictability of growth and the guaranteed minimal returns and it is a powerful asset that must be considered. But how powerful **is** life insurance as an asset?

Let's do some basic calculations of increasing complexity to illustrate. The proprietary research contained herein is the exclusive work of the Unique Minds Consulting Group, a wholly owned subsidiary of The Lamp of Castle Holdings, Inc. It may not be reproduced in any way. Current research may be licensed and shared with your clients, contact Joe Templin for details.

Treynor Ratio:

Wikipedia defines the Treynor Ratio as "a measurement of the returns earned in excess of that which could have been earned on a riskless investment (i.e. Treasury Bill) per each unit of market risk assumed. The higher the Treynor ratio, *T,* the better the performance under analysis due to the higher after tax return per unit risk."

$$T = (R - r)/\beta$$

Where R is the return of the portfolio, r is the risk-free rate of return, and β is the beta of the portfolio in question.

Utilizing twenty-year portfolio dividend historical data provided by a major Life Insurance Company as a representative example and the 90-day Treasury Bill as the risk-free benchmark, we derive a Treynor ratio of 4.52. By comparison, the S&P 500 has had a Treynor Ratio of -0.210 over the same time, the Russell 2000 has a value of -0.110, LIBOR comes in at -2.623, and the Wilshire REIT Index has a Treynor Ratio of -0.092 (calculations by Muller). It is important to note that the portfolio betas for these five assets are all positive. LIBOR was used as a substitute for a bond index since the

134

disappearance of the Lehman Brothers Bond Index.

ASSET	TREYNOR RATIO
Cash Value	4.52
S & P 500	-0.210
Russell 2000	-0.110
LIBOR	-2.623
Wilshire REIT Index	-0.092

Sortino Ratio:

A Sortino Ratio calculation utilizing the previous data sources yields an even more impressive measure of downside only risk: if the required minimum threshold return is set at the historical cash return level, one can see that after adjusting for acquisition charges the insurance portfolio returns have exceeded the hurdle rate every single year for multiple decades.

Wikipedia states "The Sortino ratio measures the risk-adjusted return of an investment asset, portfolio or strategy. It is a modification of the Sharpe ratio but penalizes only those returns falling below a user-specified target, or required rate of return, while the Sharpe ratio penalizes both upside and downside volatility equally. It is thus a measure of risk-adjusted returns that treats risk more realistically than the Sharpe ratio. The Sortino ratio, *S,* is calculated as:

$$S = (R - T) / DR$$

Where

$R \equiv$ Realized return of portfolio

$T \equiv$ Target rate of return for investment strategy

$DR \equiv$ Downside Risk

The target rate, *T,* was originally known as the minimum acceptable return, or MAR. The downside risk, *DR,* is the target semideviation

= square root of the target semivariance (TSV). TSV is the return distribution's lower partial moment of degree 2 (LPM$_2$).   DR is equal to

$$\left(\int_{-\infty}^{T} (T-x)(T-x)f(x)dx \right)^{-1/2}$$

Where T is often taken to be the risk-free interest rate and $f(x)$ is the probability density function of the returns. Thus, the ratio is the actual rate of return in excess of the investor's target rate of return, per unit of downside risk."

Calculations (by Muller) utilizing the previous data with the same assumptions yields:

ASSET	SORTINO RATIO
Cash Value	Infinite
S & P 500	-0.238
Russell 2000	-0.137
LIBOR	-1.967
Wilshire REIT Index	-0.116

The infinite result of the Cash Value is because the insurance portfolio has never failed to meet the minimum threshold of the cash benchmark in historical review, and the negative values for the assets in this analysis are due to their not exceeding the minimum acceptable return, which was taken as the mean of the tax-adjusted return of the 90-day US Treasury Bill. The superior returns per unit of risk assumed clearly and with mathematical rigor shows that cash value life insurance is an excellent asset as part of a client's overall portfolio.

Muller-Templin Simplification Ratio:

The introduction of the Muller-Templin Simplification Ratio (P_{mt}) allows a quick and dirty "back of the envelope" calculation as favored by engineers. As there are tax considerations that create additional leverage opportunities, the After-Tax MTSR (P_{amt}) addresses the issue by applying a simple delta factor for tax effects, reducing returns where applicable by the long-term capital gains rate in place when these calculations were derived (a conservative assumption to be sure).

The ATMTSR, P_{amt}, of an investment, is defined as:
$$P_{amt} = \{100\ r\ (1-R)\} / \sigma$$

Where:

r = *portfolio return*

R = *tax rate*

σ = *standard deviation of the portfolio return*

For simplicity and conservativity we assumed a flat 20% rate for all assets that do not enjoy explicit endorsement in the US Tax Code. Real world taxes are higher and progressive for most assets and have fluctuated significantly over the past thirty years. This tax leverage is especially valuable for clients in the upper tax brackets.

The following results were derived:

ASSET	*Pamt*
Cash Value	3.227
S & P 500	0.394
Russell 2000	0.980
LIBOR	1.585
Wilshire REIT Index	0.132

The superiority of Cash Value is intuitively obvious to the most casual of observers. Planners who do not consider the usage of the Cash Value asset as a risk mitigation technique for their clients create unnecessary risk.

APPENDIX B: Language

Belief and confidence will take you far. But like the difference between someone that barely makes the big leagues and a perennial Allstar is slim, so too is the difference between building a marginally successful financial services business and a great one that year after year is winning accolades and clients. One edge of excellence is your language, and like physical skills should be practiced to the point where it is forgotten because it is muscle memory as opposed to a conscious thought.

All of the language in this Appendix is a combination of Joe's language he used as a financial planner, our research over the past decade plus, and things we have blatantly stolen from other financial advisors that we recognize as useful for you. If you have additional suggestions or questions send them to us at info@unique-minds.com.

On Practice

We are both 4th Dans in Tae Kwon Do. We were not handed these belts for our movie star good looks, nor because our parents gave tons of money to a black belt factory. We bought these with our sweat. In the old old days a new practitioner was given a white belt with their uniform. Over time the belt became stained with sweat and dirt, turning yellow then brown. Dried blood is very dark, darker than the dirt and so the once white belt eventually over the years would turn almost black. After formal testing for admission to the highest levels, the student would receive a new belt, a black one signifying the knowledge achieved via sacrifice. You would also receive a white belt to signify the start of a new learning journey.

Over the decades the black belt would bleach out from the sun, and become frayed, turning white over time as the teacher continues their journey of learning. Think about this for a moment please.

Another example of practice is the world of music. The old joke of "How does one get to Carnegie Hall?" "Practice, practice, practice."

There is a highly successful Rep (Tom Lipscomb) who lives in that thriving metropolis of Shawnee Mission, Kansas. And he writes well over a million dollars a year of premium. Tom's secret? He has a Masters in Saxophone Performance. Tom practiced his scales for an hour every day for decades as a musician. He has applied that same focus on repetitive excellence and focus on detail to his language as an Advisor and is unparalleled.

Joe's cello instructor was first chair in a major orchestra as well as head of the music department for a college. And as he ingrained in Joe "If I don't practice one day I notice. If I don't practice two days the critics notice. And if I don't practice three days in a row, the public notices." Are you this committed to daily practice? You should be, if you are deciding to build a successful financial services business.

Dr. Stolk has fired more rounds of ammunition than a small police department. He has also been fired on. So he is literally cool under fire because he is experienced with it. He is alive today because he practiced to the point where he did not think, he just did. You need that level of competence in your business if you decide you want to be great.

Game time is NOT practice time. Professional athletes do not just show up and play (Allen Iverson could have

141

actually won a title if he practiced). How many months does a fighter train for a few minutes in the octagon/ring? How many swings is a baseball player taking in the cage, for four or five plate appearances a game? How many times do you practice your language for that one chance in front of the client that can write a $10mm check?

Joe had a fish in his office. Every single day he asked that fish for introductions. EVERY. SINGLE. DAY. He never got an introduction from that darn fish, but he averaged over 30 introductions a week for over a decade because of the practice. Are you getting that many introductions? Maybe asking a fish for introductions is not such a crazy idea then….

We are going to skip HOW to practice until the end of this section, because we want you to review the language first.

Phoning

We are going to assume that you have introductions to begin with. If you are not working 100% on an introductory basis, review the section on referrals and get on it, because as Joey Davenport (President of The Hoopis Performance Network) states: cold calling is God's punishment for Advisors who haven't learned to get referrals.

So here is the actual phoning language Joe used to become a 90%+ phoner. And no, he is not supernaturally gifted as a phoner. In fact he hated it and hates it to this day. He used to not have a phone in his apartment (back when people actually still had land lines) because Joe hated the phone so much. He hated phoning so much he would break out in sweats before dialing. So he became awesome at phoning to minimize the amount of time he had to do it. Using the following language, Joe was able to get his phoning time down to under 15 minutes a day. Worst 15 minutes of his day every day, but it was the most critical part because without dialing he'd have no one to do financial planning with. So become excellent at phoning so that you have more meetings, thus more people helped, and ultimately more income and impact.

Assume that Joe is the financial planner, Dr. Karl Umstadter is the referror, and Dr. Tim Finnegan is the potential client.

"Hi, is Dr. Finnegan available?"

"Speaking."

"Dr. Finnegan, this is Joe Templin, am I catching you at a bad time?" (If yes, Joe would ask when would be a better time and call them then. This is showing respect, which in turn will earn you respect.)

"No, I can talk now."

"Is my name familiar?"

"No, it's not." (Answer is almost always no. If yes then your job is much easier and you can skip the next interaction.)

"What about Dr. Karl Umstadter?"

"I work with Dr. Umstadter."

"Ah, good. Well, Karl said that I should give you a buzz, that we should sit down together at some point. What tends to work better for you Tim, morning or afternoon?"

"What do you do for Karl?"

"I'm Karl's finance guy. But he really wanted you and I to get a chance to meet because he likes and respects you and figured that you and I should get a chance to meet, so that you can understand who I am and what I do, in case you need my network or knowledge at any point. Is earlier in the week or later in the week better for you Tim?"

"Is this about insurance?"

"Could be if you want it to be, as I am a financial advisor. But Karl just wanted us to get a chance to meet as I have really helped him and he values your friendship and opinion. He thinks that we might hit it off and at some point I might be of value to you like I am to him. With that in mind, are you more of a morning or afternoon guy?"

"What is it you do?"

"I'm a financial advisor Tim. But the main reason I am reaching out to you is Karl mentioned some good stuff about you and suggested we connect because it might be mutually beneficial down the road. So at this point Dr. Umstadter thinks that we should get a chance to sit down and get a chance to meet to start laying to groundwork for a relationship. Is late morning or early afternoon typically better for you?"

"Late morning is generally better."

And now you are in the process of setting the appointment. They will probably "dance" with you a bit until they get it in their head that you want to start building a relationship, based on what the person who introduced you has said about them. Everyone is a bit jaded these days, and there are too many people in financial services that are just focused on trying to sell something as opposed to helping the client, so this is part of the bias that you are going to be fighting. If the Referror hasn't done a good job teeing you up you will need to ask three times or more, if they have done a good job you will only have to ask once or twice as the relationship and respect of the person introducing you clears the way.

By giving them choices as to when you can meet (A or B), the potential client feels like they have control. Avoid Yes/No answers after the opening exchange (when you actually use No/Yes to cut through the initial tendencies to be in a position to have a conversation). Make the choices narrower in scope, then TELL them when you will meet. For example, the following illustrates funneling the potential client from meeting at any time to a specific one of your choosing:

Is early week or later week better for you?

Is morning or afternoon better?

I have Thursday at 8:30 and Friday at 10:00 open right now. Which do you prefer?

OR

Is early week or later in the week better?

Is Monday or Wednesday generally more doable?

All I have on Monday next week is a 2:30. Does that work or should we look further out?

Note that the implicit assumption is that they are going to meet with you. It should literally be a surprise if they won't meet with you (unless they are already working with someone from your firm), because the mental programming you should adopt is that everyone wants to meet you because you help them out so much.

Now there are some external studies that show that the longer a potential client stays on the phone with you, the higher the probability they will schedule an appointment with you. This is not to say that you should try to keep them on the line for a half hour, but the longer you actually carry on a conversation with the person on the other side of the phone the greater the reduction in their mental defenses, especially if you keep reiterating the referror's name so that subconsciously the potential client is tying you and them together, thus allowing the positive relationship between Referror and potential client to work in your favor. You might want to check "The Art and Science of Trust" by Joe for some insight on this.

Also note that Joe actually answers Dr. Finnegan's questions, but then always brings it back to meeting because Dr. Umstadter says that they should. Dr. Umstadter's name is what opens the door. And Joe uses the term "but" because it creates a mental break and discounts the phrase coming before it, thus placing the emphasis on what comes afterward. This makes the potential client's subconscious focus on the name of the person that introduced you and that because of them you would like to meet. Dr. Stolk is currently writing a book explaining the underlying neuropsychology of this.

After the second or third iteration Tim will start to realize that you want to meet him, not sell him. Failing to ask at least three times (in a pleasantly persistent not offensive manner) is one of the reasons for low reached to appointment ratios as it normally takes three times hearing a fact or idea that is contrary to be accepted by the mind.

One of the things that you might notice if you were to re-read the above interaction is how frequently we use the Referror (Dr. Umstadter)'s name, and connect the Referror to the potential client. The stronger this relationship, the higher the probability of setting the appointment. If you were to call either John or Joe and use the other's name as the person suggesting that you call, you would get the meeting every time because of the mutual respect. Getting strong introductions will improve your phoning ratios, so you might want to go and review the section on introductions to help with this aspect of your business.

Approach

Here is a prototypical approach that Joe actually used all the way up to his last full-time day as a financial planner. The words may evolve over time, but it is the belief in the concept behind them that is critical.

Keep in mind that successful people are generally busy and have no time to brook fools. So respect their time, and demand that they respect yours. You are not here to be their friend, even though friendships often do develop over time. You are here to determine if the potential client and you are a good fit in terms of needs, abilities, resources, and philosophies. You are not paid by the hour, but for results. Keep that in the back of your mind and focus on doing the right things for the person, and you are more likely to do business and develop a friendship because you are being intellectually and emotionally honest.

Without further ado…

"Mrs. Rodriguez, it's nice to meet you. We are both busy professionals and so I won't waste our valuable time. Did Dr. Frankenstein tell you about what my staff and I do?"

They will either respond with a variation of Yes, or a variation of No. Quite frankly it doesn't matter, because **I** am in charge. It is MY meeting. I will continue to give them the illusion of control, but just like a Master fighting a novice I am controlling the entire encounter. Subtly. Let them think they are in control, while in reality you are because you are asking the questions.

If they say "No", my response is "Great, let's take a few minutes for me to explain so that you and I are on the same page." If they say "Yes" I would respond "Great, you are a half step ahead. But let's take a few minutes to explain in my own words so that you and I are on the same page." Either way, I am going to (using our model from phoning) acknowledge what they say BUT say what I want to make sure that they here ME explain, so that there is no ambiguity and I maintain the position of power.

"What I do is help people. And I use the financial planning process as the core method to achieve this mission of helping people. I will help you to figure out in greater clarity where you are now financially and where you want to go, what you want to achieve. This ranges from everything to helping you retire when and how you want, sending the kids to the schools you want whether Harvard or State, starting a business, or charitable works. And we look at it under multiple scenarios, so no matter what unexpected events happen in the interim you will still be able to do what you want. This includes looking at what you have right now, both through work and the planning you have already done. If you are on track for your goals great, but if not we look at what changes we need to make so that you are ultimately OK and can achieve all of your goals and objectives under any scenario. Some of this might involve changing investment allocations and strategies, it might involve getting legal documents drawn up, it might mean saving more or purchasing insurances or even just standing pat. I have no clue until after we talk so that I can understand where you are and where you want to be.

Once we have figured out the best course of action for you we need to implement the solutions. Some of these might require external experts such as attorneys or other professionals, some of it I can put in place for you. If there are solutions to be implemented that I can do it is only fair to do so with me, wouldn't you agree? (If they disagree discuss this with them until they realize that you do create value even if they do not buy a product from you. Use analogies like discussions with other professionals to make them understand and appreciate your value.)

So what I ask is that if you can look yourself in the mirror and say "Joe has helped me" without any doubt, that you agree to help me grow my business. When I create value for you, I ask that in return you introduce me to other people that I can take through the same process and help, the same way that (Referror) introduced us. And if I don't help you then I haven't earned the right for introductions. But just like I helped (Referror) with my financial planning process, I am sure I can help you in the same manner. Is that fair and reasonable? (Get them to verbalize "Yes".)

So you agree to proceed with our financial planning discussion and to compensate me with introductions when I add value, or save you taxes, or find you free money that benefits you and your family, just like (Referror) introduced us, correct? (Get them to acknowledge this again.)

Good, let's proceed then. What is your full legal name, and what do you prefer I call you?"

The next thing I do is reinforce the illusion of choice for the potential client.

"Is there anything particular you want to make sure we talk about today?" I do this because if they have a particular question or need, ignoring that issue will instantly disqualify me from working with this person because their sub-surface need that has boiled up is the most important thing in their Universe. More important than my process, more important than anything else. But asking this naturally helps put them at ease so we can have the discussion that we need to have to help them. Make sure you write down what they want to talk about, and tell them when in your discussion today you will address it ("we'll get to that in about five minutes" or "let me grab some additional info before we get to that, ok?" or "as we talk today, I think the answer to that might reveal itself"). Keep to your process, but find a point a bit into your meeting where you can address their concern. Then look them right in the eye to make sure that they are getting what they need, because then you will get what you want out of the meeting.

Notice that throughout the Approach we ask the client questions to get them involved. There is a lot of psychology involved in this that we will reveal to you, but understand that getting the client to say "Yes" to you often and early in your discussions will subconsciously prime them to continue to say yes throughout your process, including when you ask them for introductions or to ultimately purchase a product from you. Getting them to verbally agree makes them hear themselves agree with you, which creates greater commitment for the client and increases your probability of success.

You should alter the above approach to make it fit you better if there are certain phrases that are very "you", or the specifics of your situation are different (e.g. firm requires you to use particular disclaimers, you are working with a specific profession, etc.). Make sure you make the language your own as it will be much more powerful!

Other approaches that could make sense to use in different situations include:

1. The Evil Knievel/Civil Engineer: Mr. Client, my job is to reduce risk and increase certainty that you will reach your goals. Here, let's draw a picture. (Draw a chasm, label left side "Present" and right side "Future"). On this side we have where you are today, with your job and family situation and current finances. And over here we have where you want to be whether it is retirement, funding kids' educations, or what have you (write these on right). Now, in the middle is the Gap of Uncertainty. How do we get from here (point to left bank) to here (point to right)? (let them answer) Well, we could go all Evil Knievel and try to jump from here to here (draw ramp and motorcycle), but do you realize how often he crashed and burned, and broke every bone and nearly lost everything? So you probably say "That's not a great plan." But too many people that we both know leave getting to the other side to a wing and a prayer and luck, hoping everything goes perfect until they reach the far side. Remember that the only physical law as powerful as gravity is Murphy's: stuff will go wrong, at the worst possible time. Look at the stock market and job market right now! Better than planning on being lucky would be to call on the experts and design a nice bridge from here to there (start drawing a bridge) that can handle the winds that might gust up, or the quakes that could shake our world here, or whatever other outside events could prevent you from reaching your future over here. A nice safe bridge, well designed and strongly built out of quality stuff instead of the lowest bidder. Would you agree this is a better way to get from here to here (pointing)? My job is to work with you and find out how big the gap is to your goals, design the right bridges to get over the gap, and then build and maintain the bridges so that you can smoothly drive to the other side and reach your goals. Would that work for you? (This works well with engineers because you are somewhat speaking their language without getting uber geeky.)

2. The Tom Hagen: For some reason Italian-Americans seem to love "The Godfather" movies, and with good reason as they are great cinema. So if you are working with a hard core Italian American business owner this discussion works very well, especially if you are Irish German like Joe is and they have a picture from the movie on their wall. Ask the client if they know what you do, and no matter what they say respond with "Actually, my job is to be your Tom Hagen. You know Tom, right? The little Irish German kid that Sonny brings home in The Godfather who becomes adopted into the family? (let them answer with "oh, yeah, yeah!" or something along those lines) He is not in the "family business", but is the guy with the knowledge and degrees and relationships to help make everything right for the Corleones. He sits at the table with them, helps them with strategy and planning and to try and not do anything stupid, and then he goes and helps put people and assets into place. I want to be your Tom Hagen, your Consigliore. I want to help you and your family make the right choices. And it starts with us sitting here, having a cup of coffee, talking about your family business."

3. Add and Subtract: Works awesome for families with young kids. "Mrs. Client, would you say your life is more hectic now than it was five years ago? Why? (LET THEM ANSWER!!) In addition to (re-iterate some of what they said), there is the changes in the tax code, and the investment world, and the insurance landscape. The tax code is approaching one hundred thousand pages. The investment world changes as often as a diaper. And there are more insurance products available now than there were people in my home town. Quite frankly, the financial world is pretty much chaos, would you agree? (let them answer) Now, do you think that things are going to get better or worse over the next five years? (answer) Are you going to have more time to deal with this or less as your kids get into school and soccer and everything else? (answer) My job is to add to your peace of mind and certainty and balance sheet by reducing the chaos, at least in a small area. By bringing some clarity to your financial situation I can literally take the insurance and investment problems off your plate so you can deal with the scraped knees and sick kids and school projects and other things that happen all the time. By adding me and my firm into your life, you basically subtract all the worries about this stuff because it is my job to pay attention to them and lets you pay attention to raising your family and building your career. Would that be helpful?"

4. The CEO: This works very well with anyone with an MBA or that works in an organization where they understand the corporate structure. Draw an org chart for them, with CEO at the top.

"This is you. You are the CEO of your life. Right now you are really a startup, which means that you have to handle everything: finance, HR, benefits, legal, accounting. (draw circles with all of these under the CEO). Maybe you can handle it all right now, but given the complexity of each of these areas and how quickly they change, it doesn't really make sense for the CEO to be doing all of this all the time, because you actually need to be doing your job of living your life and doing your real job. So my job is to be your COO (Chief Operating Officer). (Draw circle with COO under the CEO and have all other functions connect to this circle). I coordinate all of these other functions like insurance and accounting and finance and benefits. I look at the current situation, what the rules are, and where you as the CEO are taking us with your strategy. I then either put in place the right plans like in insurance and investments, or work with the experts in these lines like the accountant and attorney, and coordinate everyone to work for the boss: you.

The key to the approach again is to communicate who you are, what (and how) you do it, and how you get compensated. You need to make sure that you are speaking a language that the client will understand so that you can work with them; using unfamiliar high finance terms and jargon would be like speaking Chinese while using engineering concepts to try and explain the world to a French painter. Speak in the client's language and couch what you do in a way that they can understand or else your financial planning relationship with them is going to be really short.

5. Straight to the Point: My job is to help you reach all your financial goals. I have no clue what they are yet, so let's talk about them and see how I can help you.

Fact Finding Questions

The feeling finding component of a Fact Finder is where you should invest your face to face time with the client to understand them so that you can guide them. Your firm probably has a form that they require to provide a basic level of analysis, that has the information required for whatever computer program you are to be using (and that your Compliance Department will sign off on). Look at those questions as a minimum.

The following questions are ones that we have found should be asked during the fact finder to truly understand your potential client:

Thinking back, did you always want to be a (whatever they do for a living)?

How did you get where you are today (in the work world)?

Where do you see yourself going with your career?

What are the next few steps for you work wise?

So when you aren't in the office, how do you spend your time?

How did you pay for college? What would you like to do for your kids?

What does retirement mean to you?

What financial issues keep you awake at night?

What does "rich" mean to you? What about "OK"?

Notice we aren't asking for their 401k statements here or copies of their trusts or employee benefits book. Those are all important hard data (facts and figures) information that is required to do the right job to assist the client. That is the factual basis of their financial situation, but it is a wildly incomplete picture.

Other questions Joe asks to potential clients include:

ARC of Life: When we sit down 10 years from today, what does it say on your business card, if we are still using them? Are you still with (insert firm name)? What do you see your title as? What is the family situation then? Where do you believe you'll be living?

When we sit down at that ten year point and we look back, what do you think is your biggest Accomplishment?

At that ten year point, what do you feel could be your biggest Regret? If we can help prevent that from happening, would our professional relationship be a success?

Now, looking out to the future ten years from now, what do you think your older self's biggest Concern for the future is?

Memory:

If you ask your client about the past, they recall the memory and embed you into that memory when re-stored. So one thing to do is get them to express memories that are important for their future. These also make them Associate you with their successes and finances, thus having them increase their trust of you per the Trust Factor. Questions that do this include:

What is your earliest and/or strongest memory of money growing up? How do you think that impacts your philosophies today and your decisions for the future?

What do you feel is the best decision you've made financially, and why?

What have you had to sacrifice to achieve success?

When did you first take control of your financial planning? Tell me more about that please.

If I could give a message to 22 year old you, what would it be to bend the curve for your future?

What sort of memory and legacy do you have from your parents/grandparents? What would you like your children/grandchildren to say thirty years from now when asked the same question?

Closing

Closing should be the easiest part of the entire financial planning process. The client should ask you "How do we get this to happen?" If you have to fight them and twist their arm, you haven't done enough understanding and revealing with the client, because the motivation to move forward should come from within them.

That being said, there are some classical closing techniques that are actually very effective. But before we get into them, a word on the difference between closing for insurance and closing for investments. Investments are sexy, insurance is pretty boring. Insurance also has much more emotional baggage attached to it, because the client's cousin's brother's sister in law's dog groomer once had a bad experience. Make sure that if the client is going to go down this path you discover it during your fact finding and neutralize that crazy talk. Do so with logic ("Insurance isn't a religion. It's like science. You don't have to believe in it for gravity to still work. And just like all those apps on the phone, you don't need to know all the intricacies of how it all functions, you need to ask if the companies we use are reliable or buggy.") and with emotion to neutralize the negative emotions.

The **Medical Close** for insurance ("it is going to take a week or so for the med stuff to get done, then we need to make sure that you even qualify for the coverage because XYZ Company has high standards and you might not qualify...so let's just start this process to see if it is even an option as part of the plan") is very powerful and effective.

Another good close is the **Term to Perm Close.** It goes along the lines of: look, if you get hit by the beer truck crossing the street this weekend, (spouse) won't care if you had the basic term coverage or the absolutely best permanent coverage with every bell and whistle known to mankind. They will just ask one question: will we be ok? My job is to make sure that I can look him/her in the eye and say "Yes", and know deep in my soul that what you want for them will happen. I don't care what type of coverage you get right now, but long range I want you to do the most efficient thing. And I want you to have peace of mind. So let's get the coverage in place now so (spouse) doesn't have to worry and do it as term. We will escrow the higher amount for the next 2-3 months so you have the habit of setting it aside but are not obligated to do so. Then when you say "aw, that's no problem" we can exchange the term for the stronger permanent, and you have the cashflow adjustment built in."

Take it Away. If you literally take something away from someone they want it more, because they either have to work for it, or it is forbidden, or they have to prove themselves. Slide the recommendations away from the client, saying something along the lines of:

"If you are not sophisticated enough for this, that's ok..."

"If you aren't going to be above the tax threshold, we don't need this type of planning..."

"I'm only accepting five clients this quarter, and sense you don't seem that interested..."

"Or if you want your kids to take extra loans for college so after they can't..."

"But since you can't trust your own judgement and mine..."

"I don't know if you qualify for..."

Make them want and prove to you! Make them sell you on why they should be your client instead of the other way around.

Remember the old saying: something is neither good nor bad until compared to something else. So use the **Compare Close**. Which isn't really a close but a concept, where you make sure you invest time with the client on a compare and contrast basis. Basically the principle power behind Dr. Martin Luther King Jr.'s "I Have a Dream" speech is the dream versus nightmare, the good versus bad of the world, the back and forth between the opposites so the listener can truly comprehend the two sides and decide which they want.

Compare Close is NOT looking at the features of X policy or investment versus Y, but the big picture stuff. What will the world be like if there is no coverage versus coverage? What does little Suzie's future look like post college with $2k a month is student loan bills versus none because they saved? What will happen if Mom enters a nursing home at the cost of $15k a month, or needs your spouse to spend every day caring for them versus purchasing long term care coverage? Get them to see and feel the future one way versus the other. It is more powerful than any cheap closing technique you can learn in a book.

Introductions

Your process for getting introductions is:

1. Let them know you will ask for them once you have earned the right to do so by creating value.

2. Create value in your process (every step of the way).

3. Ask for introductions.

4. Make it easy for them.

This is a process that should be repeated with every single person you take through your planning process. IF you are doing this you should average over three introductions per meeting kept, which will provide more than enough fuel for your financial planning machine. This is the single most important component to build a successful financial services business. Unless you like cold calling for hour after hour and feeling your soul sucked away.

Cold calling is for people that like to get punched in the face again and again and again. As martial artists we have learned that not getting hit is better than getting hit, not because of the effect of any particular punch or kick but the accumulated effect. Repeated blows to the head cause brain damage. If you get hung up on or told NO! one hundred times a day (which is the threshold to survive in a cold call environment), either you are a masochist or it will suck away your will to live and self-esteem. It will literally damage your psyche to try and survive just by cold calling. It also wastes time, because all the studies have shown that working on an introductory basis is many times more effective than cold calling.

You can literally be told NO one tenth as often while building a more successful practice and business if you transition to introductory based relationships with clients. That is probably a much more efficient and fun way to go about your career. But if you want to continue to buy the same lead lists as everyone else or call the people in the paper having babies and buying houses, feel free. Knock yourself out, since you have about as much chance of success as pulling the Ace of Spades from a deck. While you are at it, just go to the casino and put it all on 00 on the roulette wheel and get through your misery and go broke quicker, as you have about that much of a chance of building a great financial services business if you are cold calling for appointments. Might as well stand on a street corner and ask everyone that walks by "Hey buddy, wanna buy some life insurance?" because it will be about as effective.

So we think we have you convinced that working on a referral or introductory basis is a much better way to go than the cold call route. So how do you get the introductions in the first place? Even if you have been in the profession for a little while we suggest that you go back to the beginning: most people in our field start out by talking to their friends and family. Have you at least offered your services to everyone that you care about? We suggest starting here with the caveat that your friends and family are lousy clients. Not that they aren't good people or that they have a need and might even be economically in a decent position, it is just that they ARE your friends and family. If you try to use language that is not what they are used to hearing from you they will proclaim it a canned sales pitch. They will make comments like "Didn't know you'd clean up so good", and make fun of your tie. If you recommend something they will probably project memories from your shared past into the suggestion or discussion, thus preventing them from seeing you as you are as opposed to how you were. And they will ask you questions at the wrong time, like when you are at a family picnic or a hockey game. But they are important people in your life, so you should at least offer them the opportunity of your service.

Offer to take every member of your family and each of your friends through your process so that you can explain and show them what you REALLY do, to dispel any misconceptions and to make sure that they are OK. To make sure that you can sleep at night, knowing that you at least gave them the opportunity to benefit from your knowledge and guidance. **Remember that it is about you helping them, not the other way around.**

Most will say NO, but you have to realize that they are not saying NO to you the professional of today, but to the disconnect between the professional you today and the buddy from college that they have embarrassing photos of, or their snot nosed little cousin following them around in pigtails. If they cannot separate past from present reality do not hold it against them; at some point they may see the error of their ways and seek you out.

Just make sure that your friends and family are ready to pay your price for going through your financial planning process. And your price is this: if and when you provide value to them in your process, they will introduce you to other people that could benefit from talking to you. **You work strictly on an introductory basis.** Tell them up front that this is a condition of working with you. Since they obviously like you, they will agree. So then you can take them through your process, earn the right to ask for introductions by adding value to them, and then you ask. It literally is that simple to start building a referral based business.

To re-iterate, your process for getting introductions is:

1. Let them know you will ask for them once you have earned the right to do so by creating value.

2. Create value in your process (every step of the way).

3. Ask for introductions.

4. Make it easy for them.

Because it is SO critical that this process is imbedded in you and becomes second nature, we will restate the process in slightly different terms yet again to help you adopt it.

ONE: Right up front when you are setting the expectations for your professional relationship, tell them that you work on an introductory basis and that IF you add value to them (say by saving them taxes, or helping them understand their retirement situation, or by referring them to another professional) you WILL ask for introductions as compensation for your time.

TWO: Create value for the client. Good fact finding should uncover numerous situations for the client such as the fact that they need more money to pay for the college that is increasing at inflation plus two percent per year, or that getting into their employer's 401k will get them 3-4% per year of free money, or that their job search was tax deductible. There are literally too many potential value points to cover in this book, but you need to educate your client and point out situations to them to help them as well as get them to reflect upon their decisions and philosophies in the financial world that they do not truly understand. Then you will have done something worth a tremendous amount to the client, and as such you deserve to be paid. And you are paid in introductions to other people you could potentially help.

THREE: ASK. We will give you some phrases that you can use, but literally if you have created enough value (which the potential client acknowledges) then you can be horrible at actually asking for introductions yet still succeed simply since clients will willingly introduce you to others because of the expectation and experience you created. Ask and ye shall receive. And ask EVERY time you add value (initial appointment, presentation, policy delivery, review), because since you brought value you deserve to be compensated.

FOUR: Make it simple. Clients are lazy, because they are people. You need to make it extremely easy for them to introduce you to others because they don't want to expend the mental energy to do so. Some easy things you can see yourself doing:

1. Do your R&D (research and development) before your meetings so that you can have feeder lists for the clients. Linkedin is the perfect cyber stalking tool, as could be their corporate website.
2. Ask them to pull out their cell phones and open the contacts, or pull up the last ten people they called.
3. Bring up the names of their co-workers that they mentioned, or use the categories of where they used to work or where they went to school.
4. What do they do when not working? Who are they with?
5. If they have kids, who are the kids' friends' parents?
6. Who are their children's godparents? Are they godparents to anyone?
7. What about their siblings, parents, family?

Another thing to use is the concept of "Money in Motion". Because the human brain is programmed to notice movement/changes (hence the flashing strobe in the red traffic light, to grab your attention). These are people that are marrying (divorcing), changing jobs (including first job or retiring), buying/selling a home or business, having kids/kids graduation. These all produce changes in the financial situation that could use a professional like yourself to give them guidance NOW, and everyone knows someone going through these situations. We will include the exact language at the end of the appendix.

Make sure you always do your pre-work. Five minutes of prep work will give you a handful of introductions every single time, guaranteeing that you will continue to have people to talk to and build your business with.

Now some Reps we have worked with have said "Well, I am going to wait until they buy something from me because I haven't added any value until then." Hogwash we say! Bunk! If you in your initial discussion with the client get them to reflect upon why they are allocating their investments the way they are and have them take some form of risk tolerance questionnaire that shows their assets are out of alignment with their philosophies, that is valuable. If you get them to discuss WHY paying for their children's education is important to them, that adds value. If you show them that they need an additional two million dollars of insurance coverage to have their family stay in the same home and school system the way they would want, that is worth something. A fee based planner would charge $200+ per hour for this guidance, as would a therapist or attorney or accountant. You are a bit of all of these rolled into one, and you are helping them.

Therefore you deserve to be paid, and paid for every meeting because they might opt to not continue in your process. So if you are waiting until they buy something from you to ask for introductions to pay for your time, you will be paid less than 15% of the time. That is no way to run a business, definitely not a successful one.

So ask for introductions every time that you have an interaction with a potential client or client that brings value to them. The consistency of doing this is critical because it literally trains people to be good clients, and eventually they will show up for a semi-annual review with a list of typed referrals for you as payment for helping them. And that is exactly what you want: well-trained clients that will build your business by introducing you to potential clients on a regular basis in sufficient quantity that the law of large numbers works in your favor.

So how many introductions do you need to have a high probability of success? There are really two answers to this question: a starting inventory of names and an ongoing replenishment of your inventory of introductions. As to how many names you have to start, more is better. If you have 100 names and one tells you NO!, that is one percent of your inventory that is used up. If you only have twenty-five names, one NO! is 4% of your inventory, a major concentration that makes every single name critical and reduces the effect of probability as your ally. But if you have 300+ names to start then each one is only a third of a percent of your warehouse. And if the Granum Ratio applies (10:3:1), then this initial bankroll of 300 names will translate into 30 new clients, a good start to your career (or re-start as the case may be). **So 300 is the minimum starting number of names.**

Joe has seen too many talented new agents with a ton of potential start, sell 40 policies in under six months, and then be gone because they did not replenish their inventory by getting more introductions at a high enough rate to replace what they were burning through. Let them be a warning to you as we don't think that you want to be successful for a few months but rather for a few decades or more, and consistently getting high quality introductions is critical to this.

So how many introductions do you need on a regular basis? If you are being told NO on the phone 100 times a quarter after your initial ramp up, you need at least four times this many names to process as roughly 50% of the people you try to contact you will be unable to. Of those that you do reach, probably 50% will set appointments with you (note, not all of them will keep their meetings with you), meaning only ~20% of the names you get in any time period will translate into appointments. **So as a new Representative you should be focusing on getting 400 introductions a quarter to maintain the growth of your business**. This will translate into eight new Fact Finders a week, thus producing the 2+ new clients for the week that will get you to success.

If you have been licensed for more than a quarter of a year you might think that we are insane to set the referral requirement at this level. You might be thinking that you would kill for that many introductions in a year, let alone a week. We say thirty a week because it is just the mathematics of the situation. As a new advisor your phoning ratios and appointment kept rates will be lower than a more experienced Rep, and as such you need to push more people through your process to guarantee you have sufficient output.

Less than four introductions a day in your first few years and you will never be able to have the activity level (three kept per day minimum) that is needed to guarantee you survive and thrive in the business, and even at that level there is a lot of doubt. Harness the law of large numbers to work for you. Five plus introductions per day should maintain enough inventory for you to not have to worry about having enough people to call, typically one of the greatest fears of a new advisor.

120 introductions a month will minimize your call reluctance simply because even if someone tells you NO they represent only at worst one half of one percent of the people you have to contact, so you are too busy helping other people to dwell on one person not wanting to meet with you.

Having at least five new names enter your system a day will keep your business thriving and you mentally strong as you will know that you are doing the right things to hit Million Dollar Round Table and Court of the Table.

Even if you aren't there yet, you are doing the right things to get there. Let's say for example that you are only keeping about five appointments per week right now because you have been cold calling and not asking for introductions every time you meet with someone. At this level you are probably not super busy or very happy, because you have lots of wasted time in your business day, and you get hung up on a ton when you cold-call people for appointments. How can we transition you to working on an introductory basis and get enough of them to make you succeed?

First, make a list of those that have actually bought from you and go back to them. They are trusting you to take care of their families with the planning you have done and the policies you have put in force, so they should be ready to introduce you to others as long as you train them to do so.

Second, schedule reviews with these clients (or do the following when you deliver their policies, or have your already scheduled next meeting with them), and be ready to have the introduction discussion with them. You might want to go back a few pages and review the process of gathering introductions (tell them you will ask, earn the right to ask, ask, and make it easy) so that you are ready to take these clients through this process.

If you were to start doing this with every client then you would see a huge jump in the number of referrals you were getting each week. A doubling or tripling of your introductions is not uncommon for those that start doing this consistently.

Putting some numbers around this, let us use our five appointment a week kept friend from above. If they follow the process (tell them you will ask, earn the right to ask via adding value, ask, and make it easy for the client by giving them names and categories), you should be getting over three introductions per kept appointment. These three introductions per appointment yield 15 for the week to begin, a significant jump from where you are now.

These fifteen introductions will over the next quarter increase the weekly number of appointments kept by about one per day (simultaneously increasing introductions to over 25 per week) to the point where you have transformed yourself into an introduction gathering, appointment keeping, asset collecting, policy generating machine in under three months. Your overall activity won't be to the level you need to guarantee success yet, but the growth over the quarter is tremendous.

If you then continue to grow at the same rate by using the same processes, at the end of six months you have completely transformed your business and will be able to maintain a healthy growth rate.

What would your business and life look like if you were to grow like this?

Is it better than where you are now?

Introductions are the material that you build your client base from. Having a process to acquire your raw material makes sense, and ensuring that you have a continuous flow of high quality raw material will help you build a high quality business.

More of Practice

Now that we have gone over language, let's review the importance of practice.

Practice does not make perfect. Focused practice makes perfect. Think about that. Don't half ass your practice because you'll get blown up in the game.

From Joe's Tae Kwon Do Master he learned that it takes 100 times doing a technique to "get it", a thousand times to get it right, and 10,000 times to master it. How many times have you practiced your phone language? Probably under 100. So don't get upset with your results, get to work. Get those reps in, to be a great Rep.

Hall of Famer Lenny Moore summed it up: amateurs do something until they get it right. Professionals practice until they can't do it wrong. Do you want an amateur surgeon working on you?

So here are some techniques for practice that you might not have thought of.

1. Write it out. Don't type it, write it out old school. Why? Your body can't tell the difference between hitting the "c" key on a keyboard and the "2". There is no haptic feedback. But when you write a 2 your body knows what it is. It ingrains in your mind better because of the feedback. So write your language out a few times a day when it is new to you, and a few times a week when you are experienced. Eventually you can almost write it out without thinking while watching TV. This is the mastery you seek.

2. Record it. The human voice is powerful. Your OWN voice is the most powerful. Record your language and play it back several times a day. After you start really having it down you can have other stuff going on (like listening to music or watching a game) because it is reinforcing a message you have heard.

3. Solo practice. This is like what Joe did with his fish.

4. Role Play. Work with another advisor to pretend you are really doing the language. They can throw real objections at you so you need to think and react closer to a real-world situation when compared to prospecting the fish. It is more like a live fire exercise in the military or sparring in martial arts. Almost a friendly scrimmage. And have your partner give you feedback.

5. Watch the tape. Record yourself doing your language so you can see and hear it, thus making alterations. This probably scares the poop out of

you, unless you've been a successful athlete because you are used to the feedback loop. If it scares you, it is probably a good thing to do…

As you can see we move up in complexity and intensity as well as effect. Just like a black belt starts as a white belt but still practices those basics, just like the professional musician still practices their scales as a warm up, so too should the planner review their basic language before going into use it.

Money in Motion

There are particular times when people tend to be overwhelmed by a situation that is both quick in occurring and different from what they have experienced before. It is during these times of transition that professional guidance is most needed and least often sought because of the chaos. These are the times I am of most value.

We call these key situations "LifePoints" as they are regarded as among the most stressful in a person's life, as involve critical financial decisions that should not be made under emotional duress but need to be made. I help reduce the fear at these times and give an experienced and reasoned guidance. Sometimes we call them "Money in Motion" because of the changes that are going on. Both work.

The first is **change in job situation**. For our firm's youngest clients this is their first job, for other's it is switching jobs. There are new benefits to understand and integrate, maybe changes in cashflow, and old investments to move so that everything stays organized. And if there is a move it can trigger additional needs we could assist with.

Two variations on the job situation are clients retiring, which is a one shot to get it right scenario. As is selling their business, as both of these involve a tremendous amount of emotional stress on top of the financial decisions.

The second LifePoint is **change in marriage** situation. The first obvious one is getting married, where suddenly there is a co-dependency of finances and new restrictions on beneficiaries and the like. One of the leading stressors in marriage is miscommunication about finance so that is one area our firm does a lot of work in.

And unfortunately about half the marriages in the US end in divorce. The unwinding of finances and QDRO's and insurance needs radically change, often mandated by law. We help here.

And unfortunately, some people are widowed. This might be the single most stressful situation in a person's life. I can't tell you how many widows and widowers my firm has helped, and we are always thanked for this.

A third LifePoint that is common is **buying or selling a house** or property. Banks often mandate some of what my firm can provide.

Fourth is change in dependents. Having a child, adoption. Kids going off to college is a big emotional and financial change too that we address. We all want to do right for our kids, and our planning lays the groundwork for those kids' futures.

Last is large influx. We have many clients on Wall Street who get huge bonuses that we help deploy, as well as stock option money. Inheritances and lottery winners actually make up a decent chunk of our business too. Lottery winners are very likely to declare bankruptcy, almost as likely as former pro athletes because they just don't know what to do with so much. We help them figure it out.

So let's talk about these five (hold up hand, fingers spread) LifePoints and how I can help these people.

APPENDIX C: Resources

There is an old story about Albert Einstein. Someone asked for his phone number and he went to the phone book to look it up. The person said something like "Herr Einstein, you don't know your number?" to which he replied "No, I never call myself. But I know where to find it!"

So we are including some of our favorite financial services resources for training or information so you know where to find it. This is obviously not an all-inclusive list, but it is a huge amount of information for you to tap into.

Web Based Sources:

The Life and Health Insurance Foundation for Education (LIFE): You might have heard their radio commercials "Beep. Beep. Beep. Beeeeeeeeeeeeeeep. Life insurance isn't for those who die, it is for those who live." And other ones like it promoting the purchase of insurance. LIFE is a non-profit focused on educating the public on insurance. As a totally independent source they are a smart group to tap into.

In addition to having lots of great educational pieces, LIFE has an entire series of videos called "Real Life Stories" on how the purchase of insurance of various forms has helped families and businesses across the country. These are not paid actors, these are the actual people telling the story of how the disability insurance kept them in the house or the life insurance kept the business going or the long term care prevented the old lady from becoming destitute. Both the clients and the agents speak in the clips so these are among the most motivational things you can ever watch.

LIFE also is the force behind both Life Insurance Awareness Month (LIAM, or September) and Disability Insurance Awareness Month (May). Tapping into these campaigns can do nothing but good for your business.

The LIFE website is www.LIFEhappens.org

National Association of Insurance and Financial Advisors: www.naifa.org

The oldest organization specifically designed for agents and advisors can provide you lots of excellent resources. In addition to the magazine Advisor Today (also available on-line), the website has an almost limitless supply of information and resources. NAIFA members share their best practices and sales secrets freely with one another, so the collective wisdom of others is available to you via the meetings.

NAIFA membership allows you to put the logo on your business card (if your Company allows it, which almost all do), which can be an opener for discussions leading to a lot of business. Joe wrote hundreds of thousands of dollars of premium just because of that little blue triangle on his card.

Hoopis Performance Network: www.hoopis.com

Developed by industry legend Harry Hoopis as he faced mandatory retirement as a General Agent, HPN has evolved from a way for Harry to keep busy and help a few Advisors in retirement to one of the greatest training platforms available. HPN delivers video based training in vignettes by tapping into industry leaders from hundreds of companies and disciplines. Everything from basic mental toughness to advanced estate planning concepts, Hoopis is one of the most complete training supplements available.

We would recommend watching at least one clip a day, every day. You will literally never use up the knowledge feed that Hoopis provides. Check to see if your Firm has a corporate relationship with them in place.

Pete Grieder:

www.petegrieder.com Grieder is a shrink that Northwestern Mutual used to help coach field management, and had a lasting impact on Joe's development in management. He is a former sports psychologist for the Orlando Magic and has worked with the US Chamber of Commerce.

Million Dollar Round Table:

The MDRT website is www.mdrt.org. Every day they have a power phrase that will help you. Several of them for this year are actually taken from other books by the authors.

The Million Dollar Round Table is the benchmark for the industry. It represents the top ~10% of the profession across the world. MDRT should be your minimal acceptable threshold of production (roughly $200,000 of gross production in 2017), with Court of the Table (~$600k of production) really being where you want to be.

MDRT provides tremendous resources including a bookstore, mentoring programs, speeches from some of the most influential financial services professionals to ever walk the earth, and productivity tools for your business. If you have made it to MDRT level of production you should consider joining and learning what you can to reach the next level.

The Introduction Machine:

www.introductionmachine.com

Since introductions are the raw material that you process to be able to fuel your business, anything that you can do to ensure a continuous stream of high quality people to talk to reduces the risk of your business and directly translates into cash flow for you.

The Introduction Machine is actually a cell phone based app that you can give to your clients and prospects that will reside on their smart phone. When they are hanging out in the bar with their buddies and the talk turns to money and they say "You should talk to my guy/lady! They're awesome!" typically that is the end of it and you as the Rep never know about it. The introduction gets lost. But the Introduction Machine captures those introductions in the bar, at the gym, wherever your clients are and talking to people.

It works because your client can text their buddy, and instantly that person has your contact information. More importantly, you as the agent get an email saying "Juan Smith shared your contact with Suzie Riley. Contact phone:XXX-XXX-XXXX." Let us repeat that: you get an email with all the needed information about the person you were just referred to and by whom.

In addition to the live capture of these introductions that would be lost, the website has marketing plans, language, and psychology lessons to improve your introduction gathering prowess. If there is one skill that will determine your long range success, it is your ability to prospect for gold by getting high quality introductions, and The Introduction Machine can help.

If you are reading this still then you are probably very interested, and should be rewarded. The code "2WEEKTRIAL" will get you a free two weeks to try out the Introduction Machine so that you can start integrating it into your business.

Tom Hegna: www.TomHegna.com

If you ever get a chance to hear Tom speak, do so. His breadth and depth of knowledge from his time as not only a producer but as a senior executive is truly impressive. His book "Paychecks and Playchecks" is the single best resource on how and why annuities work. Period, no debate.

Tom's website has lots of economic insight and language and selling concepts and so makes a nice supplement to this book, and is cost effective too.

BOOKS!

Back before the internet (when dinosaurs roamed the earth according to our kids) we used these things called "books" to learn, to capture the wisdom of others.

What follows is a list of some of our favorite books. Some directly relate to building your financial services business, but most will do so indirectly. A few are just fun.

This is our list so it is obviously totally biased. It also will evolve over time, and we look for suggestions as to other books to add in.

The Art and Science of Client Building, by Al Granum The guidebook for building an insurance based financial services business. Very technical but will give you the minutiae of greatness in our field.

The Art of War by Sun Tzu

Probably the most widely read book on military strategy, The Art of War has influenced military leaders as well as business owners for hundreds of years. It holds secrets that will help you, if you are ready to expand your thinking.

The E-Myth Revisited, by Michael Gerber:

The people run the systems, the systems run the business. How to build a process driven organization that delivers consistently great results.

Financial Mistakes of Young Americans, by Joe Templin: the finest in edutainment for financial services. This is literally the client focused side of the first decade of Joe's business. If you were to hand this book to your younger clients (or the 20 something's that are your client's kids), you would get them on the right path fairly easily.

Following Through, by Levinson & Grieder

Good intentions won't get the job done. Why is the gym empty by March? Why don't people achieve their goals? Read this book and get some tactics to re-inforce your willpower.

The 4 Hour Work Week   Tim Ferriss

The original guide to ultimate leverage and enjoyment. Not fully applicable to the financial services world due to regulations, compliance departments, etc., but reading this book will change how you think about what you do. And never be afraid to fire a bad client!

The 33 Laws of War, by Robert Greene

Military principles from across the centuries, applied to life and business.

Do You Want to Make MDRT, or Not?   Stolk & Templin.

One of the greatest training books ever written. Because we say so.

The Greatest Salesman in the World, by Og Mandino.

Parable of the secret to success in sales. Easy read, an oldie but goodie.

How to Win Friends and Influence People, Dale Carnegie

One of the most seminal works that continues to be a best seller today.

No Necktie Required   Juli McNeeley

First female President in NAIFA's 125-year history, Juli has built a successful financial services practice in Wisconsin. Oriented towards the female advisor, his book is valuable to anyone that ever talks to a female. Plus Juli has broken ground beyond her gender.

Pay Checks and Play Checks   Tom Hegna

The most definitive work on annuities. Buy it, devour it. Give it to your clients. Your production will jump!

Pitch Anything by Orrin Klaff

An investment banker by background, Klaff has literally raised billions of dollars for companies and projects. He has invested even more time than we have into how the mind works from a sales/buying perspective.

Taking the IF out of Life   Shane Westerhoelder

Twenty-five years in financial services including running a coast-to-coast full service firm have given Shane some good insights.

The Tao te Ching, by Lao Tse

The Tao is like water. Powerful, flowing, life giving. Read the book to understand the power of doing by not doing.

Think and Grow Rich, by Napoleon Hill

Some not great stuff has come out about his life, but this book is one of the earliest to talk about harnessing the power of the mind to influence your outcomes.

The Trusted Adviser   Maister, Green, & Galford

A pretty deep read, definitely not for the brand new Rep. But excellent to help you evolve beyond the plateau you may be stuck on.

SOME RANDOM STUFF

There are a lot of other random things out there to help you. Instead of trying to organize and go really in depth, we are going to shotgun some ideas and maybe some will stick.

Music

Joe listened to the Theme From Highlander ("Princes of the Universe" by Queen) every single morning between his gym and his office. Guys in kilts with swords. Gets your heart pumping. Try it, and listen to the lyrics and ask how they apply to our field of financial services.

The Hallelujiah Chorus from Handel. Can't hear it and not be inspired to go.

Eye of the Tiger. Dun, dah dah duh. Enough said.

What song gets you amped up and ready to fight? Why aren't you playing it each morning, to flip the switch? If you were to play that song, how would you feel? Would it help your outlook? What about your performance?

Visuals

Humans are highly visual animals. Use this to your advantage.

Write your goal on a post it note. Put it on the fridge.

Draw a smiley face on a post it note and put it by your phone.

Make a goal thermometer and have it in your home so you and your significant other can see it. Make sure they know what it means, because they will ask you about it regularly.

Use pennies on your desk to count down daily goals (introductions, new appointments on the phone, whatevs).

With a client, take out your phone, turn it on "do not disturb". Place face down on the table, then lean forward and talk.

Sign your name in a green pen.

Keep your desk almost but not totally clean.

APPENDIX D:

Biz Planning and Documents

"Those who fail to plan, plan to fail." This has been beaten into our heads from our earliest moments in our careers, and it is true. A corollary to it though is the saying from Mike Tyson "Everyone has a plan until they get punched in the face." You need to have a plan, and you need to adapt on the fly. As Dr. Stolk will tell you: no military operation goes exactly as planned. Ever.

So you need to do as much work on your plan up front as possible. Not going into the microscopic necessarily, but understanding as much as possible the variables and accounting for them. Because Murphy's Law is more powerful than anything else.

Just like the financial plans you assemble for your clients should address multiple potential scenarios (death, disability, underperforming markets, etc.) so too should your business planning (loss of key employee, shifting market conditions and regulations, outperformance, time off for personal training, etc.).

As we talked about with the Ideal Calendar Day, it isn't going to happen. But having the most well-grounded yet flexible plan to achieve the objective will reduce your anxiety, increase your overall performance, and force you from a Producer to Business Owner with the benefits that accrue.

We cannot out of necessity give you everything you might need here: that would be like you handing a client the entire Internal Revenue Code: overwhelming and ultimately useless as it is too much. But here are a few things that our experience has shown could probably help most of the people reading this. These were created by the Executive Counsellor Guild with input from Unique Minds, and you may use them in your business. For more powerful tools you might consider talking to Dr. Stolk, he can be reached at info@ec-guild.com.

Effective Business Planning

Business plans by financial necessity set a broad target for success of a company without knowing the mechanics of the day-to-day work or practical challenges of running a company.

After the business plan is written, owners find that their beautiful plans do not fit what happens in the real world. They discover the difference between business plans and the game plan, the difference between the ends and means. They all too often have focused on grand strategy and ignored the tactics. They discover the necessity of adjusting the means by which your operation heads for its goals.

Game plans grow out of business plans. Get from one to the other by gradually bridging the gap and bringing into focus those things you must do to reach your goals.

The focusing process is where we start.

Note the progression: Set the strategy in your business plan and tactics in your game plan. We go from the theoretical to the practical by monitoring and managing. Big picture to minutiae.

B. An Obvious Sports Analogy

Every coach knows you don't win games in the locker room by drawing up beautiful plans.

On the field, beauty doesn't matter as much as the score. You win if you know what it takes to win and execute. In a game, this means outscoring your opponent. In business, it means many things: making money, dominating markets, providing products and services of value to your clients, making a contribution to society, and giving others the opportunity to achieve success and security. In financial services, it is selling products, acquiring assets, and retaining the clients.

Does a coach call the next play without knowing where the ball is located? No more than you can make a good marketing decision without knowing who your clients are now.

You must know where and how the actual experience of your company deviates from the projections in your business plan: financially and in your marketing and sales efforts. You must know where you are in order to get where you are going before time runs out in the game.

Most business books are cheerleaders-they offer support but little direct help. You can draw energy from dreaming about your billion dollar Asset Under Management organization. Whether you get that far depends on how well you plan and execute.

In business, as in sports, planning and executing are everything.

C. Business Plan is Integral to Success of the Game

Plan:

- Less than 42% of small business started operations with formal business plans.

- Among business with revenues less than $500,000, only 1 in 3 began with a formal plan.

- Among companies with written business plans, 40% found their projections so optimistic as to be useless once they began their operations. Most of the others found their plans so incomplete as to be ineffective. Only 2 of 3 used balance sheets or profit analysis in their plans.

- Two in three small companies found their plans lacking because the plans did not consider the factors most importing to running a growth company: finance, marketing, product development and operations.

- Many small business owners in the survey attributed their success to investments in technology, employee training or marketing, and not to any business plan. However, among small businesses that experienced growth over two years, 59% based operations on a formal plan; 79% attributed their success primarily to this connection.

- Roughly 11% of Financial Representatives pass 5 years with their initial company.

D. A Greater Prosperity

Few financial planners or small businesses focus on long term planning, or more importantly on implementing their plans. If they did, they would likely enjoy greater prosperity.

Once you are established and have evolved past the Survival stage of business and are ready to Transition from a financial planning PRACTICE to BUSINESS, you will need to truly operate like a business to avoid plateauing and even regressing. Dr. Stolk created the Business MRI to address this issue we see all too often,

From **The Executive Counsellor Guild Business MRI:**

"A specific example of the benefit of planning by small businesses is the increased accuracy of financial projections. Accurately predicting income allows small businesses to create realistic and achievable programs for growth and expansion. No business is too small to have more profit.

Systems dependent businesses rather than people-dependent businesses which add value to company in a number of ways ... generally produce more with higher profit margins. Without a plan you may falter because it's hard to make good decisions without a framework."

Business plans, as a rule, don't address critical issues, like communicating your goals to employees and customers. They formulate broad goals, but they don't tell you how to set your business up day to day so as to reach those goals. They don't tell you how to implement your business plan and measure your performance. They serve the needs of a different audience: bankers and investors. They don't help the day-to-day players who execute your game plan: coworkers, clients, vendors. If your business plan is not on target, you won't get funding.

Contrast this to the financial planning world, where usually the only business plan based pitch is to your management.

E. Guiding Principles

The success of the plan depends on how well the leadership of the company solves everyday problems. That means you as the financial advisor, because in addition to being the salesperson you get to manage staff and do all the other stuff until you grow to the point of having a full team.

- Set standards and give employees the tools to meet goals; measure if standards are being met.

- Lead by example (focus on the ratios and measures you value). Don't leave early for stupid things.

- Find the important details and focus on them. Know the details of your business and which details are critical. Study your business and extract those details critical to your success.

- Data is about quantity: Measure performing by asking objective questions.

How well do our results match up against our expectations; what's different; is the trend up or down; will these trends last a short time, or do they look long term; what might have contributed to what we see in the data; what's missing from this data that would lead us to ask more questions.

If you are not recording data about everything in your business (like via SAMUSA as we recommended), you will either fail, or drastically underperform and wish you had been keeping data. Again, your choice.

Finance is devoted to quantitative analysis-measuring the results of your efforts. Because in the end we are all capitalists in this field. It is "financial services", not "feel good services". Finance provides data from which you draw the benchmarks for measuring your company's performance.

- Face reality when you look at your company data

- Variance may mean trouble, so keep an eye on it. Your business may outperform your projections or fall short. Either way, you need to know. A game plan allows you to monitor performance in detail, so learn how performance varies from the vision of your business plan.

- There are no shortcuts in preparing the information, in studying it, in acting upon it. Analyzing the data takes time, at least twice as long as it takes to compile it.

Just as many problems can arise from outperforming your expectations. Are you prepared with staff and resources to accept faster growth than you initially projected? Take each variance as an opportunity to rethink each aspect of your business. Recognize how changes in growth affect your business.

F. Effective business planning

Vision statement: Expresses what the company wants to be in the business world, the endpoint.

Mission statement: Expresses what the company does to achieve its Vision. The mission statement tells your employees what your company will do in order to reach their goals.

Vision Statement

What does your business look like down the road? What are you working for every day, sacrificing to build?

1. What do you see your company becoming in five to ten years?
2. What are your values?
3. What will your customers be looking for?
4. Draft of your vision statement.

As an example, Joe's was "A decade from now, the Tech Valley Financial Network is the premier financial planning organization in Saratoga and the (Company Name Removed) system. We have dozens of the most ethical, productive, and credentialized professionals in the world doing creative work for great clients and friends."

Ask yourself:

Does your vision statement answer these questions:

1. Who are you as a company?

2. Where do you want to make your mark?

3. How high do you want to shoot?

4. What do you believe in?

5. Does what you have written embody the spirit of where you want your company to head?

6. Can you live with this vision? Are you willing to act in accordance with your vision?

Mission Statement

The Mission Statement is short and powerful, like a shot of whiskey. It should be the essence of what you and your firm DO, distilled down. As an example, Joe's mission statement was "We help people. We help people clarify and achieve their financial goals and dreams." It is direct and succinct, but leaves some interpretation open. Joe's entire team knew and lived this Mission Statement, as should you and yours.

How do you create a Mission Statement? Start by asking:

1. What do you sell?
2. To whom do you sell?
3. What does your company/you do better or want to do better than anyone else?
4. How does your company rank the importance of quality, value, and service?
5. How do you define each of these based on customer

needs and expectations?

6. How will you achieve your vision?

Draft of your mission statement, ask yourself:

Does your mission statement capture what makes you unique as a company?

Would your clients, managers, and providers recognize you in these statements?

Would they be pleasantly surprised because they could really buy into these directions?

Is your mission statement inspiring?

Does this give everyone in your office a direction for each day when they walk in the door?

Is there any ambiguity in what is most important?

If an employee faced a difficult dilemma at work, would thinking of your mission statement lead them to make the right decision?

Would your grandparents understand what you do?

Key Success Factors

There are certain factors that will predict successful outcomes. Understanding these Key Success Factors is critical.

Activity

Activity is the precursor to productivity in financial services. We know that the core activities will drive the business to success. It makes sense to draw from previous year's activity and productivity to develop the appropriate ratios.

Examples of Key Success Factors for Activity:

1. One new Fact Finder a day with a family earning $300k or more.
2. Four Introductions per day to individuals above the Roth Contribution limit.
3. Present one retirement plan per week.
4. Present three long term care cases a month.
5. Sell $5mm of term insurance a month.

If you have not already done so, calculating the following ratios will be important to your success:

Introductions : New Client

Revenue per New Client

Revenue per Existing Client

Dials : Reach

Reach : Appointment

New Scheduled : New Appointments Kept

Old Scheduled : Old Appointments Kept

New Appointment Kept : Case Open

Case Open : Presentation (Close)

Closes : New Client

Once you understand your ratios determining the Key Success Factors to achieve your goals is fairly basic. Again, tracking data is critical to long range success, and ratios that are out of whack with norms reveal skill issues that can be addressed via coaching. If you chose to ignore data collection and ratio analysis, you have made a choice to leave your success to chance.

Key Success Factor #1:

If we_____ then we will be successful.

Key Success Factor #2:

If we_____ then we will be successful.

Note we focus on one or two activities only (preferably a daily and a weekly/monthly) as too many will split attention.

As an example, Joe had a daily Key Success Factor (1 new appointment a day on the phone) and one weekly one (1 new client submitted per week). Consistently hitting these would drive his business to the production he wanted. The short cycle feedback loop allowed him to continuously achieve and succeed or adjust.

Human Resources/Staffing:

Your team is what determines your success. Achieving greatness in financial services as a solo practitioner is no longer viable due to compliance related paperwork and the complexity of the financial planning process. Delegate, empower, develop, and review to grow.

Key Success Factor #1:

If we _____ then we will be successful.

Key Success Factor #2:

If we_____ then we will be successful.

You can and should look beyond these two areas for your business's health and growth. Other areas you may consider:

      Marketing

      Recruiting

      Educational Development

      Cross-Selling

      Development of Centers of Influence

      Client Service

      Expense Management

      Compliance

SWOT ANALYSIS

"He who knows his enemy and himself will always be victorious in battle. He who knows either his enemy or himself will be taste victory only half the time. He who knows neither his enemy nor himself shall ever be conquered."

The Art of War

Strengths:

Weaknesses:

Opportunities:

Threats:

Ask Yourself:

- Do these action items work toward meeting the set objective?

- If all the action items under a single objective are met, will the objective be met?

- Are these action items clear enough to give yourself and employees adequate direction?

- Is there any ambiguity about what successful accomplishment means?

- Are you committed to getting these things done?

- Do you think these plans are realistic given your current workload?

- Do you have the full buy-in of all stakeholders (support staff, your management {including compliance officer}, and your family)?

5 Stages of Business Development

If you have read the first book in this training series (Do You Want to Make MDRT, of Not?) then the following diagram should be familiar as it was the inspiration for our cover. It is a representation of the Five Stages of Business Development as that first book really was focused on getting those brand new to the financial planning or insurance/investment world through the Inception (or Initiation) and Survival Phases and to start the process of Transition. Which is where this book starts and then brings you beyond.

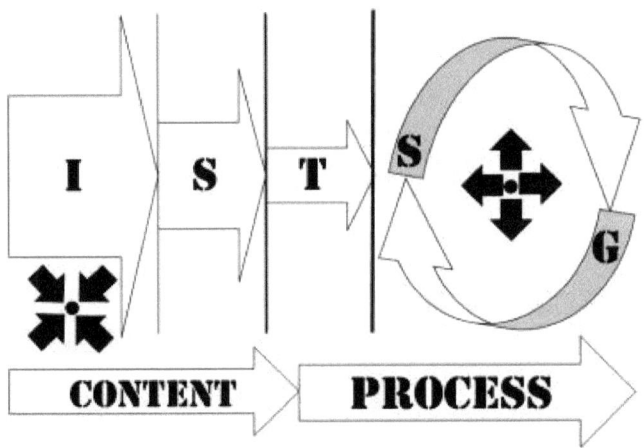

The first three phases are linear, typically described as the entrepreneurial phases, and are expert/sales centric. The last two phases are circular and more externally focused.

Initiation Phase

This is the phase when the expert entrepreneur decides to start a company to sell their product or service. It is common for this phase to be completely product or service centric. In the financial services world this is when you start working with clients, and start selling. You sell, or you starve.

The entrepreneur projects their enthusiasm and fascination on the prospects of success without properly investigating marketing research and/or developing proper business engineering in order to create the correct business structure for the current stage of the enterprise.

The majority of "companies" get through this phase without operating with a real business plan beyond "sell and sell more". The quantity and quality of the output of the business is totally relying on the individual (you) that happens to execute the task at hand. You sell and Survive, or you fail out. It is fairly simple.

On average about sixty percent of companies will survive the Initiation Phase. In our world though it is about the same: 50%-60% don't make it to six months. This is the "drinking from a firehose" stage, and many drown. Just focus on seeing as many potential clients as you can, and master the arts of getting introductions and appointments if you want to make it past the basic licensing and first field work stage.

Survival Phase

This phase is described as "when everybody is doing everything" within a manufacturing or similar company. In our world it is "you". You call clients, do paperwork, follow up with underwriters, do the filing. ALL of it is on

YOU.

Many commission runs you don't have a check.

There is usually a lack of mid- and long term planning. Short term planning is essentially "whatever hits the desk today" and "whoever I can try to sell" and "put out the fire". You are building your basic skill set, trying to figure out who at your broker dealer to call to make sure you have the right forms, and trying to make sure you have gas and parking money to get to the appointments. While trying to sell.

On average about twenty percent of companies (including financial services) will get past the Survival Phase. The average timeframe, for other industries, is three to five years and average revenue is below two million. For the financial services world you escape here at roughly twelve to eighteen months (75 policies sold, $10mm AUM acquired, or $125k investment gross in trailing twelve months {or a combo of these}). More in higher cost areas.

But if you can adopt an activity driven process model as we have laid out, you WILL make it as long as you are seeing enough potential clients and working diligently on yourself.

Transition Phase

The last of the linear phases is the most complex and difficult phase. The company needs to transition from an entrepreneurial company, where the owner(s) still micro manage to a company where the owner(s) can be absent without impact on the company operations. This is where the realization sets in that having employees based on personal relationships (friends and family) is not the right reason for employment. It is time to understand that the promotion of employees based on relationships and years of service versus their ability to perform the job function is not the answer.

In the financial services world this is where you start having staff, recurring revenue, and have your processes and ratios figured out so you are working hard plus smart and can stop running around like a chicken without a head. Typically this is around qualification for MDRT ($200k of commissionable premium, $250k of investment gross commissions, or $25mm of AUM, or a combo thereof).

The Transition phase is when the company depends on the implementation of new processes and procedures, job descriptions and controls to ensure the quantity and quality of the company's output. At this stage in other companies there are employees that earn a higher salary than the owner(s). They are often "start-up company" minded employees from the first two phases that are unable to follow the transition to improved processes and procedures and will be replaced.

During this phase old and new unhappy customers will start demanding the attention from the owner(s) and the owners will have to deal with commitments and activities outside the Company to grow and prosper the Company. Those initial people you sold $100k term policies to or invested $1,000 total for? You are outgrowing the ability to serve them.

The owner(s) will have to learn to delegate the internal management of the Company to other qualified employees. You need staff or else you will burn out, as there is too much paperwork in the investment and financial planning worlds (insurance too) to be able to do the paperwork, service clients, and acquire new clients that generate revenue to run your organization.

If the retirement goal of the owner(s) is to sell their business, it is not uncommon during the Transition Phase that the name of the business is changed to a more generic identity.

On average about twenty percent of companies will survive the Transition Phase. The average time frame is three to five year and the average revenue is below ten million in annual revenue depending on the industry. A much higher percentage of financial services people remain in this phase than in other fields, but those who do adapt and grow reach tremendous revenues and profit margins.

Summary of the First Three Phases

The first three Phases can generically be described as inward focused, reactive, and fairly disorganized (to put it mildly). Owners are working in the business, and selling is the most important thing for you. Really the only thing.

There are limited or no consequences for any actions because the only person to blame is you. You do not really have a business, at best you have a financial services practice.

Growth and Stabilization Phases

These two phases are intertwined and are more like two alternating aspects of one phase. Companies that make it to the Growth and Stabilization phases can be described as having an outward focus with a strong corporate culture. They perform yearly planning and are proactive. You set goals and objectives and measure results. Informed decisions are made based upon accurate and complete financial information. Tasks are well defined based upon organizational needs and fair treatment of employees and customers. The company will survive the owner(s) and in most cases the owner(s) manage.

In the financial services world, you have a staff that lets you focus on mainly just seeing clients. You do that and they do the analysis work and paperwork and all the "stuff". You are probably pursuing degrees like your CFP® or ChFC, actually can take some vacation and not worry that the world will collapse on day one, and you actually do annual business planning and have a handle on your ratios and projections.

Look at a well-functioning General Agency with different roles (application input, compliance, training, recruitment, etc) for an example of a Growth/Stabilization stage organization.

On average most companies that are able to transition into the Growth and Stabilization Phases will survive long term and be able to grow past ten million in annual revenue. In the financial advisory world as a solo advisor with support staff you get over $500k of annual revenue easily with a profit margin of over 50%. Seven figure incomes are not uncommon.

Review the diagram. Being in the first two stages is Hell, no way around it. You must evolve and transition through your choices to the non-linear phases, and this book is your key to doing so.

ACCOUNTING FOR NON-FINANCIAL MANAGERS

1.0   PURPOSE

1.1   This document on accounting is not designed to make you an accountant but to give you a basic understanding of some accounting terms, principles and reports so that you may run your business as a business. It is to help you build your business, and to understand/help business owner clients.

1.2   It is highly recommended that one of the relationships you establish is with a knowledgeable, respected Certified Public Accountant (CPA). He/she will be able to provide you with valuable assistance on your financial statements and with guidance on establishing a good working relationship with your new business partner, the Internal Revenue Service (IRS).

2.0   THE ACCOUNTING ENTITY

2.1   Your organization is an accounting entity. As your accountant will tell you, you must keep the accounts of your business separate from your personal accounts.

2.2   The accounts are kept in terms of money, and the math used in accounting is addition, subtraction, multiplication, and division.

2.3   The common denominator for all accounting is money.

2.4   Accounting can't tell you everything about your organization, but it can tell you more about performance and financial well-being than any other source of information.

3.0   ACCOUNTING CONCEPTS TO REMEMBER

3.1   There are three important concepts to remember about accounting.

3.1.1   Keep your business and personal accounting records separated.

3.1.2   Money is the common denominator of accounting

3.1.3   Every transaction or every accounting event affects at least two items. Accounting is properly called a double-entry system.

3.2   The third notion above made possible the following rule, to which there is absolutely no exception: "for each transaction the debit amount must equal to the credit amount."

3.3   The debit and credit arrangement used in accounting provides a useful means of checking the accuracy of the transactions recorded. This may be difficult to understand; but as entries are made, the debit/credit system will become clearer.

4.0   ACCOUNTING REPORTS TO REMEMBER

4.1   The two main end products (or reports) of an accounting system are the Income Statement (also called the Profit and Loss Statement) and the Balance Sheet.

4.2   The Income Statement measures your organization's financial performance for a period of time, called an accounting period.   You will probably spend more time with your Income Statement than with your Balance Sheet.

4.3 The Balance Sheet reports your organization's financial status at a specific point in time.

5.0 THE BALANCE SHEET

5.1 The Balance Sheet is a "snapshot" of the financial condition of your organization at a specific date. It is always dated "as of" a certain date, while the Income Statement states that it covers a certain period of time.

5.2 The Balance Sheet has two sides.

5.2.1 The left side displays the Assets. (Assets are the resources that are owned by the organization).

5.2.2 The right-side displays Equities. Equities can be thought of as either claims against the assets or the amount of funds that have been supplied to the organization from various sources and retained earnings.

5.3 The **fundamental accounting equation** is:

Assets = Equities

The double entry principle of accounting is based on this equation.

6.0 DEBITS AND CREDITS

6.1   Debits and Credits provide a very convenient way of applying the principle of double entry. They are the method in which increases and decreases are handled in the accounts.

6.2   There is another accounting equation to go along with the fundamental one above.

Debits = Credits

These two rules apply to Debits and Credits:

6.2.1   An Asset is increased by a Debit and decreased by a Credit.

6.2.2   A Liability or Equity is increased by a Credit and decreased by a Debit.

7.0   INCOME   MEASUREMENT   BY   INCOME STATEMENT

7.1   Being a profit-oriented organization, your success is reflected by increases in the Equity section of the balance sheet. The Equity section will increase by the amount of profit your organization makes. Since the Balance Sheet is a snapshot, you can see that Equity has changed but you can't determine why Equity changed.

7.2   That's where the Income Statement plays such an important role. Here you see exactly what your Revenues and Expenses were and how they affected your bottom line.

8.0 RELATIONSHIP OF INCOME STATEMENT OF BALANCE SHEET

8.1 Very simply, the Income Statement shows you the detail of why Retained Earnings (or Equity) changed.

9.0 EXPLANATION OF ACCOUNTING TERMS

9.1 **Assets:** The assets of a business are everything of value held by the business. The word value as used here means future usefulness. Cash, notes, accounts receivable (amounts owed to the business by customers), land, buildings and equipment are examples of assets in a business. An asset is recorded on the books of the acquiring entity as the actual full cost, even though it has not been fully paid for in cash. The amount of any debt or claim against the asset is included in the liabilities.

9.2 **Equities:** Equities are claims against the total assets of a business. Those who have equities in a business are the creditors (the liability holders) and the owners. A business' liabilities are owed to its creditors.

9.3 **Liabilities:** These are the debts or claims of creditors against the assets of the business. Accounts payable, notes payable, and wages owed to employees are examples of liabilities.

9.4 **Owner's Equity:** This is the owner's claim against

the assets. It is also called **Net Worth** and is the excess of total assets over total liabilities. Because creditor claims have priority over the claims of the owner of the organization, owner's equity claims are secondary (or residual).

9.5   **The Balance Sheet:** It is an expanded expression of the accounting equation

Assets = Liabilities + Owner's Equity

It summarizes the assets, liabilities and owner's equity of a business entity as of a specific point in time. The Balance Sheet is also called a statement of financial position.

9.6   **Current Assets:** They consist of cash and other assets that are expected to be converted into cash or to be used in the operation of the business within one year. Current assets are usually listed in descending order of their expected conversion into cash (liquidity).

9.6.1   **Cash:** Funds in a bank account or money held for daily transactions.

9.6.2   **Accounts Receivable:** Amounts due from customers for services rendered, for merchandise, or for any asset sold on credit.

9.6.3   **Notes Receivable:** Formal written promises to pay a fixed amount of money at a future date. Most notes can usually be exchanged for cash at a bank.

9.6.4   **Merchandise Inventory:** Products on hand and for sale. This type of inventory is found on retail store shelves and in stockrooms or warehouses.

9.6.5 **Prepaid Items:** Services and supplies that are paid for and have future usefulness in business operations. An example is Prepaid Insurance. Businesses take out insurance policies for protection against hazards. The cost of this type of protection, an insurance premium, is paid in advance. The unused portion of the insurance premium is an asset.

9.7 **Property, Buildings and Equipment:** This classification comprises assets used over a long period in the operation of a business. They are customarily listed on the balance sheet according to their degree of permanence, with the most permanent item listed first.

9.7.1 **Land:** Always listed separately. Although land and the buildings on the land are usually sold together, they are classified separately because the buildings will deteriorate through usage, whereas the land will not. Land is considered the most permanent asset.

9.7.2 **Buildings:** Those owned by the business appear on the balance sheet. Rented buildings are not owned and are not assets.

9.7.3 **Store Equipment:** Showcases, counters, and shelves are typical permanent items of store equipment used in selling the merchandise inventory.

9.7.4 **Manufacturing Equipment:** Machinery and equipment for producing manufactured products.

9.7.5 **Delivery Equipment:** Consists of trucks, cars, and other types of equipment owned and used for the delivery of products to customers.

9.8 **Current Liabilities:** This term designates obligations whose liquidation (in other words payment or settlement) is reasonably expected to require the use of current assets or the creation of other current liabilities. All liabilities to be paid within a one-year period are classified as current. They are generally listed in their probable order of liquidation.

9.8.1 **Accounts Payable:** Purchases on credit. They are the unpaid amounts owed to creditors from purchases on an account arrangement. They are usually due to be paid within 30 days and are also called open accounts.

9.8.2 **Notes Payable:** Formal written promises by the organization to pay money to creditors. Notes payable may be from the purchases of merchandise or services used in the course of business. Notes payable to a bank arise when a company borrows money for business use.

9.8.3 **Accrued Liabilities:** Since the word accrue means to increase by growth or to accumulate in a standard manner, accrued liabilities are debts that have accumulated because of the passage of time and that are not yet due for payment. Accrued wages payable and accrued interest payable are typical accrued liabilities.

10.0 CONCLUSION

10.1 This Accounting Primer is a very abbreviated introduction to accounting.

10.3   You may also find the following glossary interesting and helpful.

GLOSSARY OF ACCOUNTING TERMS:

Account: A recording device used for sorting accounting information into similar groupings.

Accounts Payable: Amounts that the organization owes to creditors.

Accounts Receivable: Amounts due from customers for sales of goods or services to them.

Accrued: Accumulated over a period of time.

Accrual basis of accounting: The basis that assumes that revenue is realized at the time of the sale of goods or services, regardless of when the cash is received. Expenses are recognized at the time the services are received and utilized or an asset is consumed in the production of revenue, regardless of when payment for these services or assets is made.

Asset: A thing of some known value owned by the organization.

Balance: The difference between the total of the debits and credits in an account.

Balance Sheet: The financial statement, which summarizes the Assets, Liabilities and Equities of an organization. It is as of a specific date.

Budget: A financial plan for a period of time.

Cash: Currency, coins, traveler' checks, checks, and any other items that your bank will accept for deposit.

Chart of Accounts: A list of all accounts in the general ledger that the organization anticipates using.

Credit: The right side of the T form of an account, the actual amount on the right side of an account, or the act of placing an amount on the right side of an account.

Creditors: Persons or organizations to whom debts are owed.

Current Assets: Cash and other assets that will be either consumed or converted into cash within twelve months.

Current Liabilities: Liabilities that will be paid within twelve months.

Debit: The left side of the T form of an account, the actual amount on the left side of an account, or the act of placing an amount on the left side of an account.

Disbursement: An actual payment by cash or check.

Double-entry Accounting: A system of recording both the debit and credit aspect of each transaction.

Entity: Your organization separate from you.

Equities: Claims against the total assets of a business.

Expense: Expired cost; the material used or service utilized in the production of revenue during the specific period.

Liability: An obligation of an organization, or a creditor' claim against the assets of an organization.

Long-term Liabilities: Debts of an organization that are not due within the current year.

Inventory: The stock of products held by an organization either for conversion into products for sale to customers or for immediate sale to customers.

Matching Concept: An accounting principle which reflects the matching of incurred expenses and earned revenue for a given time period in order to determine net income for that period.

Mortgage Payable: A debt - normally long-term - for which specific assets are pledged as securities.

Net Assets: Total assets less total liabilities.

Notes Payable: Short-term notes to creditors, much more

formal than Accounts Payable.

Owner's Equity: The owner' claim against the assets of the organization.

Prepaid Items: Unconsumed amounts of current assets that will normally be used in the operations of the firm and are not held for resale.

Property, Plant and Equipment: Long-lived or long-term assets of an organization that are used in the operations of the firm and are not held for resale.

Transaction: A business activity or event that has taken place.

Trial Balance: A statement that shows the name and balance of all ledger accounts arranged according to whether they are debits or credits. The total of the debits must equal the total of the credits in this statement.

Notes: